Finding *Love*
in All the Right Places

SHANDA Y. SMITH, PH.D., LMFT, NCC

Copyright © 2016 Shanda Y. Smith
First Edition
All rights reserved

PAGE PUBLISHING, INC.
New York, NY

First originally published by Page Publishing, Inc. 2016

ISBN 978-1-68289-597-9 (pbk)
ISBN 978-1-68289-598-6 (digital)

Library of Congress Control Number 2016942853

All Scripture quotations in this publication, unless otherwise indicated, are taken from the King James Version/New International Version Parallel Bible. Copyright © 1985, Zondervan Publishing House. All rights reserved.

No part of this publication may be reproduced, stored in a retrieval system, or transmitted in any form or by any means-electronic, mechanical, digital, photocopy, recording, or any other-except brief quotations in printed articles or reviews and other noncommercial uses permitted by copyright law, without prior permission in writing. For permission requests, contact www.findinglove4today.org.

Printed in the United States of America

CONTENTS

Introduction: A Word of Encouragement 5

Chapter 1: Finding Love in Jesus 9

Chapter 2: Why You Should Wait 19

Chapter 3: What's Wrong with Waiting? 32

Chapter 4: There Is Purpose in Waiting 46

Chapter 5: Unexpected Blessings in Brokenness 59

Chapter 6: Finding Love in Yourself 72

Chapter 7: Investing in a Healthier You 78

Chapter 8: While You Wait, Trust God for His Timing 95

Chapter 9: Final Words of Encouragement 105

Bibliography 115

INTRODUCTION

A Word of Encouragement

As I pondered upon how to begin this book, Ecclesiastes 1:9 came to mind. King Solomon was considered one of the wisest on the face of the earth. He wrote, "What has been will be again, what has been done will be done again; there is nothing new under the sun" (NIV). I took some time to reflect upon this statement. I surmise from the statement that life, as we know it, may at times have no new or surprising revelations. My mom used to say to me when I was a teenager, "Just keep living." She would say this to me when I thought I had life all figured out. Obviously, she knew something about life that I had not known at that time. And you know what, as I discovered in time, she was right. The more I matured and got older, I began to understand the full meaning of what my mom meant by those words.

As you see, we will encounter seasons and changes throughout our lives. Seasons will come, and they will go (Ecclesiastes 3:1–8). However, the one thing that will remain constant is the changes that will occur, no matter what season you may find yourself. Changes can be brought about through hardships, challenges, disappointments, and losses. No one is exempt; we will all take turns experiencing change. I will also say that change does not always mean it is something horrible. It can be something good, providing you open yourself up to the lessons to be learned. The lessons that we learn from our mistakes, failures, and disappointments can be opportunities for personal growth and maturity. Although these opportunities of growth may be new revelations for you, it does not necessarily mean they may be new revelations to others. I am sure you heard the phrase "Been there, done that." We are never alone in our experiences and can benefit in learning from each other's life's lessons. There is no mistake, failure, or disappointment that is new under the sun. As I share my mistakes, failures, disappointments, and journey in finding love, some of you may find yourself saying, "Been there, done that," while others may be embracing their moment of revelation of truth. Nevertheless, I pray the words in this book resonate with you and that you find you are not alone in your journey. After all is said, I pray you find hope and encouragement.

So who is this book for? If you have been frustrated, left confused and tired of one dead-end relationship after another, then this book is for you. In fact, I dedicate this book to all my sisters and brothers in Christ who are seeking and waiting on God for the relationship of His dreams for you (Jeremiah 29:11), not your dreams. You see, your dreams can get you into trouble and bring heartaches (something that is quite familiar to me). So what does a relationship of our God's dreams look like? Well, let me tell you. It is a relationship that is healthy spirit, soul, and body (this person is good for you and to you and you are good to them and for them) and purposeful (God has a divine reason for this person being in your life and it is not just to hang out). But, I digress.

A WORD OF ENCOURAGEMENT

I started seeking, praying, and waiting for Mr. Right around the age of twenty-four. I just knew I would be married quickly (I was delusional) and began believing God for it. Just when I thought Mr. Right found me, the relationship ended, and I was left with a broken heart, broken dreams, and broken promises. I experienced more heartbreaks and disappointments to my dismay. I had never cried so much in my life, and I am surprised that my tear ducts can still produce tears! Now, I can laugh about my experiences (Proverbs 31:25). But then it was not so funny, was downright depressing, and in some instances, was troubling. However, this finding-love thing was not going to be as easy as I originally thought.

I am forty-five years old now, and I have learned so much on the journey towards marriage. This is why I wanted to write this book. I wanted to share some of my experiences and pearls of wisdom that I have learned in my twenty-one years of waiting. After one failed relationship to the next, one thing was clear: something was not right with my choices for Mr. Right. I used to ask myself what I was doing wrong. Why is this happening to me? Did I hear wrong? Was I deceived? Did my heart lead me astray? Why do I keep attracting the same type of man? The answers to these questions you will find later in the chapters. For now, here is a hint: Jeremiah 17:9 (NIV) states, "The heart is deceitful above all things and beyond cure. Who can understand it?" As I said before, your dreams can get you into trouble because the heart may contain "issues of life" (Proverbs 4:23) that may influence your choice in finding the right mate.

With all this being said, as I grew and matured in the Lord, I realized I was looking for love in all the wrong places. I first needed to work on me. I needed to take the time to invest in me. I needed to learn to love me. You cannot love others in a healthy way unless you are first healthy yourself. I am sure you heard the phrase "You attract who you are" (meaning who you are on the inside). If you are a broken, emotional mess, a dysfunctional, needy person, that is what you will attract. It has taken me years of personal growth, discipleship classes, participating in emotional healing ministries, girlfriend talks, prayers, personal psychotherapy, and the like to reach a place of solidarity, contentment, and fulfillment as a single person. As a result, I am a wiser, happier, and stronger person. All this work led me to finding love in all the right places, myself and Jesus. Instead of looking to a man to fulfill my need to be loved and accepted, I had learned to look to Jesus, the lover of my soul, to fill these places in my heart. He is the only one that can meet this need (not even your future spouse). If I can find love in all the right places, you too can find love in all the right places! This is my charge to you.

CHAPTER 1

Finding Love in Jesus

"Love never fails."

—1 Corinthians 13:8

Have you ever heard the ole' saying (or the country song) "Looking for love in all the wrong places"? I am sure you have. When I share my story with people, I often begin with this familiar saying because essentially, this was my personal struggle and story. I can tell you that as a child, I grew up with a mother and father in the home. But for reasons unknown to me at that time, I went outside the home seeking love. Later in this chapter, I'm going to share my journey of seeking love that led to one failed relationship after another. In the process of time, God got my attention and showed me that the love I was seeking could only be found in Him, not in a man. So it is with this revelation that I tell you that the love you are looking for first begins with discovering and falling in love with Jesus. Finding love in all the right places simply means finding love in Jesus. I have discovered that there is no one on the face of this earth, including my future spouse, that can love me like Jesus. He truly loves unconditionally. His love has no boundaries, judgments, or unrealistic expectations placed on by unhealed emotional wounds. (1 Corinthians 13:1–8). Jesus's love is safe and is a sure anchor against anything. The bottom line, before you say "I do," there should be a place in your heart that has been captured by the love of Jesus. You should know him intimately and establish him as your first love, the lover of your soul. If he is not your first love, chances are you are not ready for Mr. or Mrs. Right. I can tell you that in my futile pursuit to find love (looking back on those experiences), I can see that God was jealous and zealous for my love. He wanted me to love him and pursue him in the same intensity as I was pursuing love in a man. I'll just say this. I learned that God is a jealous God (Exodus 20:3–5, 34:14). He does not like it when we put others or things before him. In essence, when we do this, that thing or person becomes an idol, and God will target it like a bull charging toward a matador in a bull fight.

In my journey of seeking love, one morning, I heard this song in my sleep as I was waking up. The lyrics of the song states, "While you wait, you might have to wait in the rain. While you wait, you may have heartache and pain. Your eyes may hurt from the tears you've cried. While you wait, your friends may not stand by your side. While you're waiting for your promises to be fulfilled in your life, remember God is never late, so just praise him while you wait." I believe this was one of God's ways to communicate with me on some of the darkest and pain-filled days of my life. The song resonated with me because I could relate to those very words. I would ask the Lord, what's wrong with me? Why did I have to suffer all those heartbreaks? Why do I have to wait so long? It seemed that my time of waiting for the promise to come was met with nothing but suffering. I began to meditate on people in the Bible that suffered. I knew Job and Jesus could relate because both were acquainted with suffering. In fact, the prophet Isaiah (53:3) said of Jesus, "He was despised and rejected by others, and a man of sorrows, intimately familiar with suffering." Moreover, Isaiah stated in 53:10 " yet it was the Lord's will to crush him and cause him to suffer, and though the Lord makes his life a guilt offering"(NIV). I learned that God has a perspective on suffering in which we cannot see at first (1 Corinthians 13:9). Job was in so much pain and suffering that he cursed the day of his birth. Job 5:18 states "for he wounds, but he also binds up. He injures, but his hands also heal"(NIV). Job and his friends did not have God's perspective regarding the reasons for Job's suffering. Satan had incited Job to God. Job was not suffering because he committed sin but because God wanted to make a point to Satan. God had confidence that Job would not deny or curse him because of his suffering. At the end, Job did just that. I can say that God did not waste any of my experiences of suffering. He redeemed, restored, and used all the experiences for my good. I begin my story in the following section.

A Shattered Heart

One day I went to lunch with a friend, and she wanted an update on how things were going with someone I thought was going to be Mr. Right. When I told her what had happened (Mr. Right ended up marrying someone else), she did not say anything at first, and then out of nowhere, she began to speak to me about Joshua and Caleb and how they had to wait a number of years before they would enter the promised land. Some of you may know this story. Joshua and Caleb saw that the promised land was obtainable and that they could go in and take possession. However, the other ten spies that gave the bad report discouraged the others, and as a result of their lack of faith, the nation of Israel had to wait a little longer to enter into the promised land. Even though Joshua and Caleb saw that the land was ripe for the taking, they had to wait years because of others' disbelief and lack of faith. But the one thing that my friend said to me was that Mr. Right's choice to marry someone else would not affect God's faithfulness for my life. God will still do it; it just may take a little longer. At the time, I knew this to be true. However, I kept wrestling with the thoughts "Here we go again. I have been here before, same script just a different face," speaking of another failed relationship.

Looking back over my life, I had boyfriends, some pseudo boyfriends (is this a committed relationship or what). But I will share only those relationships that I feel were the most impactful in this journey of finding love. The funny thing that I joke with my friends about is that none of these relationships lasted longer than six months. Just when I would get used to the idea of a steady relationship, *bam*, breakup! In hindsight, I thank God for these short-lived relationships. It kept me from more pain that I don't think I could have handled. I look back on these relationships and ask myself what I was thinking. The person I was at those times was definitely broken and emotionally messed up. You know the ole' saying "You attract who you are on the inside." If you see a pattern where you are attracting a certain type of woman or man, you have to look in the mirror and look within yourself because if you are attracting dysfunction, there must be a little or a lot of dysfunction in you. The person I am today would never ever have dated or considered these men as marriage material. I slowly begin to learn on this journey that finding love in the right place not only begins with Jesus, it also begins with finding love in yourself. I talk more about this in detail in chapter 6.

Crossing Paths

Finding love in the wrong place led me to Mr. Hollywood. Our paths crossed at a local dance studio. He was a hip-hop instructor, and I was taking classes in ballet and jazz. After some time, we began pseudo dating (you know, spending time with a person but no intention or commitment is declared). He said he cared for me, but his actions or lack thereof proved otherwise. He had been divorced from his first wife, and looking back on it, I think that the relationship affected him in terms of him being able to commit. However, he had cheated on me with another woman while he was still "seeing" and spending time with me. I stayed with him like an idiot (so naïve). Obviously, our relationship was never the same. I broke it off with him not because he cheated on me, but because I got tired of waiting for him to take the relationship to the next level. Years later, I would run into him (several times, as a matter of fact). I asked him that one question (why he would not commit to me), and he admitted that he did not know what he wanted at that time. He had gotten out of a bad relationship at that time when I ran into him and told me that he did not want to be in another relationship, ever. Interesting!

Then my journey towards finding love led me to Mr. Youth Pastor. Once again, in my naiveté, I thought since he was a pastor, I would be safe and he would be the right one. He was attracted to me, and I was attracted to him. However, his indifference told me that he did not know what he wanted. I learn that from Mr. Hollywood. I waited for him to declare his intentions, take the pseudo relationship to the next level. I got tired of waiting. We broke up the first time, got back together months later. One night he called to tell me that his mom and brothers were going out of town for the weekend (he lived with his mom and brothers) and invited me to come over and he said, "oh and bring a change of clothes. I said, what? I can't believe you asked me to do that. I am not that type of woman. I said to him you are showing your true colors" and some more choice words and then I broke it off for the final time. I found out later that he married six months after we broke up. It turns out (I believe) that he was dating this particular woman at the same time he was pseudo dating me, based on one question I asked him, which he refused to respond to. This would explain his indifference. He used to boast that when he married, he would only do it once. Several years later, I heard that she left him. They are now divorced.

Next, my journey towards finding love led me to Mr. Regret. I thought he was different. He was refreshing. We were a breath of fresh air to each other, so I thought. He had an interesting past, but I did not hold that against him. If God forgave him and was giving him a second chance at life, who was I to hold his past against him? So I got to know him. We were friends, and we talked about everything and anything. Eventually, the friendship grew into love, and we talked about plans to marry one day. I noticed over time he started to change and became emotionally and physically distant. I would see less of him. When I would call him, I felt like I was intruding. I found out that he was cheating on me with a woman he later ended up marrying. He later told our mutual friends at the time that he regretted marrying this person and should have married me. Interesting! But at that point in time, my ship had sailed. Sorry. You snooze; you lose.

Surely, I thought, Mr. Radical was the one. Long story short, he was not. We started out strong, crashed, and burned. He declared his intentions just after three weeks of dating, told me he loved me, and we began to talk marriage. Once again, I was naïve to believe that, number one, a person could fall in love in three weeks (oh brother) and, two, that the relationship was built on something solid that would lead to marriage. As time passed, he also started becoming distant emotionally and physically, meaning I would see less of him. He eventually told me that he felt God was calling him to be single and that he was called to suffer for the kingdom. At that time, I was thinking, "Well, that's okay. But couldn't you have told me this before you told me you loved me and started planning your life with me?" We broke up. One day I was curious, and I took a drive by his house (his mom's house, he lived with his mom). The Holy Spirit gently whispered, "He is a different person." I knew what the Holy Spirit was saying. We were two different people on different paths. "Hmmm, dodge that bullet, thank you, Jesus," I thought.

Mr. Spiritual, I thought, was so awesome, refreshing, and that was what attracted me to him. I had never seen a man like him. He would raise his hands, worship, see things in the spirit, pray for people, and was ministry minded. I had to get to know him. So I initiated contact with him and put my number in a card and told him, "Don't be afraid to use it." I should have never done that. That was a spirit of stupid, and you would be happy to know that I have been delivered from it. Get it? The man is supposed to find and pursue the woman, not the other way around! I found out later that Mr. Spiritual was not so spiritual. He had issues with alcohol, money problems, and unresolved emotional wounds. I learned that just because someone appears to be spiritual, it does not mean that they are mature, responsible, and ready to be a priest in their home, lead a wife, and take care of a family. I also learned that women should never initiate, ever! Remember, it is he that finds a wife, not she that finds a husband.

And finally, we come to who I thought was my Mr. Right. I will call him Mr. Perfectionist. He was intelligent. We thought the same. I got him, and I believe he got me. I understood him, as he was definitely misunderstood by many people. Some people thought he was annoying, critical, and legalistic. However, I knew and understood that deep down he was not that way on purpose. In my time of getting to know him, I discovered he had a troubled childhood, which left some unresolved wounds as an adult. Nevertheless, we were simply friends and hung out together by default because our mutual friends at the time hung out together. We were friends for about two years before we began to see each other differently. May 1, 2009, was the first time we spent time by ourselves. We were still friends at that time, nothing exclusive, just talking and discovering things and ideas in common. In time, we began to explore the possibility of being something more than friends. We were cautious, praying and seeking the Lord, and then something happened. He began to change. He also became emotionally and physically distant. I could not understand it and was confused. I expected him to "get it." After all, I thought he was a smart, intelligent guy. Well, he did not get it. Long story short, the friendship dissolved, and I found myself mad at him. Time passed, and I ended up going on a ten-day trip with my church to Israel. I found out later he was going on the same trip. "Oh brother, can I get a break?" I thought at that time. I did not want things to be weird, so I sought him out at church and told him why I was mad at him and asked for his forgiveness. He told me that he had been praying for an opportunity in which we could talk and maybe there would be an opportunity to talk in Israel. He never followed up with me. (I never initiated, learned from my experiences with Mr. Spiritual) And I never knew what he wanted to talk about. In fact, he avoided me the entire time we were in Israel. Now, I was really confused. I remember saying to the Lord, "Bring the promise to pass or release me from this individual." At that time I believed this person to be my husband. I was saying to the Lord, "I do not have to be with him." Months after coming back from the Israel trip with our church, I happened to be at the right place at the right time. It was a God moment, and I believe to this day God had me in that place to hear what I needed to hear. I overheard someone talking about Mr. Perfectionist's love story. I could not believe it. He had started dating and eventually got engaged (later married) to a woman he said he would never marry. Nevertheless, I was shocked upon hearing the news. Of course, I was sad, mad, disappointed, and grieved the loss of a dream and friendship. Looking back, as I reflect upon the experience, I am so thankful that he did not choose me. I could see that this individual was not strong and mature enough to be the man I needed. He also had some unresolved emotional childhood issues that I believe, had we married, would have affected the marriage.

What I learned was that an individual's free will does play a factor in God's will for our lives. Even if God knows the choice we would ultimately make and the consequences that come with the choice, he does not intervene. Our ability to choose is God's gift to us. God took a risk when he created us with a free will. I am grateful that God allowed this individual to choose. I believe if I had married him, I would not have been happy to this day, and our marriage would be nothing but suffering.

I took the time to share (in brief) these stories with you because I believe God had a plan for every one of those failed relationships. If you find yourself on a similar journey, God has a plan for you as well. God wastes nothing. He uses all things together for our good (Romans 8:28). As I reflect back on these relationships, I wonder what my life would have been like if I married these individuals. Quite honestly, I think I would have either been severely unhappy or divorced. God's ultimate plan for my life kept me from divorce, which would have been more painful than grieving these failed relationships. I am so grateful that these men chose someone else and not me because their choice saved me from a life of pain, suffering, and possibly divorce. I learned many things in these failed relationships (some of which I shared). After each failed relationship, God brought me one step closer to finding him, to finding true love in him. I guess I had to go through the experiences in order to know what God was trying to teach me. After my last failed relationship (with Mr. Perfectionist), God had my attention once and for all. My futile attempt to find love in a man was not working. The search for my need to be loved could only be fulfilled in Jesus alone. I needed to stop. The love I was seeking was in Jesus. This is my charge to you. If you have a void or a need to be loved, cherished, valued, wait on God. Give up futile attempts in your own effort to find love. It will just bring you more sadness, frustrations, disappointments, and heartaches. If you commit to wait on God and invest time in discovering what it means to find true love in Jesus, I promise the time spent will be worth the wait. I honestly believe that people who take the time to find love in Jesus first by allowing His love to bring wholeness and healing may have a better chance at a happier marriage and a less chance of divorcing.

CHAPTER 2

Why You Should Wait

> "Wait for the Lord; be strong and take
> heart and wait for the Lord."
>
> —Psalm 27:14 (NIV)

As you browse the aisles (or shop online) of your favorite bookstore in search of your next read, I wonder when you came across this book, did you ask yourself, "Should I read another book on relationships?" If this question came to mind, I understand. I have asked myself the exact question as I browsed the aisles of my favorite bookstore in search of my next read. I thought, "What else could I learn that I don't already know? What new insights could this book provide? Do I really need to read this book?" To answer these questions, I leave you with this to ponder: when you consider the divorce rates not only among non-Christians but among Christians as well, you may reconsider the validity of your question. I don't believe that the subject of relationships and how to find the right person is a subject that we cannot exhaust. Yes, there have been many books published about relationships, and perhaps all or some seem to be saying the same thing. However, if you have read the statistics on divorce in the past five to ten years, the message is clear: we still need work in this area. It seems that somehow we either don't know God's standards, forgot God's standards, or perhaps you know God's standards but... You fill in the blank. I know for me, the former was the culprit. I did not know God's standards regarding finding love in the right places. And let me tell you, I made some pretty dumb choices in searching (or settling, should I say) for who I thought was Mr. Right. It took years for God to reveal layers of truth, heal, restore, refine, and mature me. To me, Hosea 4:6 resonates more clearly. I get what God was saying through the prophet. "My people are destroyed from lack of knowledge" (NIV). Ever heard the saying "You do better when you know to do better"? I'm sure you have. Therefore, my purpose for writing this book is that you (we) do better. I hope that you learn from my experiences, and I pray that your "eyes of understanding would become enlightened" (Ephesians 1:18, NIV) and that God "fill you with the knowledge of his will through all spiritual wisdom and understanding" (Colossians 1:9, NIV) in regards to this issue of finding love in the right places. It is my hope that we Christians can continue to grow in this area so that we can begin to lead the world by a godly example of how to find and maintain love according to God's standards. Because of the implications for divorce in our society, I encourage you to wait until you are ready for God to bring the right person in your life.

Divorce Rate

You may think I am over exaggerating or overgeneralizing in terms of the divorce rate. I don't need to regurgitate statistics on the divorce rate in United States as well as around the world. You know them; you have already heard them cited in pulpits, platforms, journal articles, and books. What I find fascinating is that the divorce rate among Christians is either holding steady, just as high as non-Christians, or higher. How can that be? Are we missing something here? Of course, there are many factors, issues of the heart, and experiences that may be influencing these numbers. Moreover, an interesting phenomenon (at least to me) was discovered in my qualitative PhD dissertation research study. In 2010, I had interviewed eight men and eight women who had been divorced at least once (most had remarried). There were a total of thirteen questions, and significant themes were found for each question. Review my findings specifically for questions 12 and 13 below.

Table 1
Suggestions for Preparation of Marriage

ID No.	Women Question 12: Based on your experiences, describe what you perceive as essential elements or suggestions to prepare others for marriage.
	Theme: Foundation in God and premarital counseling that offers relationship expectations.
1	Make sure you understand who you are and your goals…Christ-like lifestyle…
2	Finding out who you are in Christ Jesus. Getting a solid foundation of who you are in the Lord…so you can attract healthy people. Allow the Lord to heal your heart and hurts…so you won't attract unhealthy people…
3	…Christ has to be the center of both of your lives…following Christ has to be the center of your life…but it won't be the blessing God intends for every marriage.

4	I believe in order to prepare others for marriage one must seek counseling together to learn from each other. To learn those hiding secret that need to be reveal. I believe that one must walk together on one according. Prayer is also an essential element in preparing for a marriage.
5	Absolutely essential is devotion to Jesus with knowledge and implementation of the Word forefront in the lives of both individuals.
6	In depth premarital counseling. Mandating waiting period. Pragmatic analysis of core beliefs, and a determination if these values would deter from or contribute to a health marriage. Unconditional love and respect.
7	Parents modeling good marriage (including manifest love, commitment to the individual, and conflict resolution). Parents teaching their children from an early age to love God and his ways, and how to hear His voice. Raising healthy children by loving them, teaching them to value themselves and others, and when necessary and appropriately, disciplining them. Parents and churches teaching relationship long before marriage, providing and understanding of the responsibility and importance of wisely/biblically choosing the people with whom you are going to have closer relationship and then how to affect a healthy relationship. Churches offering pre-marital counseling that deals with such things as choice, relationship expectations, shared values, resolution conflict, danger zones, loving each other, children, and more.

8	Be best friends first. Always friends—know the person in group settings, other settings. Be sure you are equally yoked spiritually. Assume nothing. Ask the hard questions while dating. Don't be afraid of the answers, and if they are a show-stopper, don't go any further.
	Men
ID No.	Question 12: Based on your experiences, describe what you perceive as essential elements or suggestions to prepare others for marriage.
	Theme: A foundation in God.
1	Two people should be equally yoked…God first, respect, consideration…
2	My answer for a successful marriage would be to have an adequate understanding of God's covenant with His people as an example of what a man's covenant should be to his wife…
3	The first is to have firm beliefs in a common world view. My new marriage is centered on our love of God, and this builds a foundation very unlike what I had before…to worship our God and further His kingdom.
4	Hearing from God, and obeying Him, Being 100% honest with each other's unhealthy thinking and behavior in the most transparent way (in front of trustworthy friends as witnesses)…

5	Get a good counselor and express your innermost feelings and desires openly, one on one with the counselor then come together as a couple and discusses these ideals. Having a mediator to help show each person their short comings and strong points, in the beginning, will give the marriage an opportunity to start out openly and without a barrage of surprises at the start. Theme: Understanding better communication and commitment to the relationship.
6	Learn to communicate with one another…
7	Communicate and be flexible be ready for change and be strong…
8	Commitment, communication, and dying to self…

Table 2
A Summary of Reasons Marriages Continue to Fail

ID No.	Women
	Question 13: In your opinion, what factors contribute to the reason(s) why marriages continue to fail?
	Theme: Lack of communication skills.
1	Lack of enjoying who you are…lack of relationship with God…lack of goals and accomplishments, no planning, no friendship, understand what marriage really means…respect one's space and ideas…

2. People don't know how to be married. They don't have the skills to prepare them for marriage. People don't understand their communication styles. People need to talk to one another correctly. Marriage is about serving and not taking. Come in expecting to serve and not take.

3. Ungodly attitudes and behavior—like adultery, lying, verbal abuse, bad communication, selfishness, bad coping skills, taking out frustrations on spouse, not being kind, understanding, and forgiving.

4. Buying into our culture's way of living, selfishness, lack of understanding, dysfunctional attachment relationships with parents during the first year of life, addictions, bondages, unresolved past trauma, baggage that is unwittingly brought into the marriage relationship.

5. In my opinion what contribute to a fail marriage is lack of communication. When marriages do not communicate it causes the marriage to become dysfunctional. I believe communication is a vital part of the marriage. I think that when you have trouble in the marriage the first thing one should do is talk about it and not keep it to yourself. Couples tend to keep things to themselves until it too late. It important to keep the communication line open concerning the marriages.

6	God not being the center of each person's life. Lack of individually honoring God's Word and ways. Self-interest and dysfunctional behaviors (sometimes narcissistic behaviors). Lack of communication skills. Man not understanding woman and woman not understanding man (different needs and ways of relating to each other and life). Different life goals. Not keeping the marriage as a covenant commitment based on God's love (agape) rather than human love (phileo).
7	Lack of forgiveness and devotion…
8	Television and movies create an illusion of what real life marriage is like. It seems that shows are either over the top in the romance or overly dramatic. Many feel that they need to have this to be "normal." Secular music often glamorizes infidelity. People often get married on a whim and realize later that they didn't have adequate time to learn if they were truly compatible for spending the rest of their lives together. Most premarital counseling is superficial at best. Divorce is too easy.
ID No.	Men Question 13: In your opinion, what factors contribute to the reason(s) why marriages continue to fail?
	Theme: God is not the center of the marriage.
1	People today must put their relationship with God first, then spouse and children…God created marriage. This is the order and he can keep it together…

WHY YOU SHOULD WAIT

2. Lack of respect for one another…get rid of self and accept God and become a disciple willing to trust and obey…marriage cannot stand without divine intervention…

3. Lack of communication, finances, and sex…

4. The Lack of communication, finances, and intimacy…

5. People fail to recognize that marriage is a union put together by God. Without Him giving direction through His word, we are left to rely on our own understanding and strength; history has proven less than satisfactory results. God's design and intention for marriage is to have life and that more abundantly. If any marriage is anything but that, it's because they are not giving their marriage to God.

6. We need to question if this is the partner with whom God wants me to be with, then won't He be with us in working out our problems…Unfortunately, marriages even based on a common belief structure will not always work with similar rates of divorce (I believe) for marriages in the church and outside of the church. Those marriages, which fail within the church are more a failure of each partner to live by Christ's words and to see their partner in the way God sees them. There are certainly many reasons for failure, but I think the same core beliefs and following the Lord are keys to success…

7	…falling prey to getting out of the habit of reading God's Word and praying together. Then after that, the most deadliest development is when one or both of the people in the marriage cease to care about what the other person is experiencing in their own heart, emotionally and spiritually, or has lost the ability to hear what the other person is saying from their heart.
8	Lack of understanding one another's needs in life! We are all wired differently… Understanding yourself is key in your personal development as well and if you know who you are you will tend to be more tolerant of others, and focus on changing you, because I can't change anyone else but me…The good part about success in marriage is that it will build your children's expectations and put them on the right foot for their families through all the generations to come.

I conclude that even the participants in my dissertation study recognize (in their remarriages) that in order to have a healthy and viable marriage, God has to remain the source and the foundation of the marriage, which means both individuals constantly working on the marriage with God at the top of triangle or God in the center. Without God (the creator of the institution of marriage) as the center or glue that binds the marriage together, there is no marriage. We are essentially functioning on our own, in our own strength and that my friends, is shaky grounds.

What Do We Make of All This?

So what do we make of all this? Allow me to elaborate for a minute. We know the United States of America to be a wealthy country in many regards, the land of the free. Many immigrants from various nations come here for better opportunities and a better quality of life. Living in a capitalist country affords us to have access to financial resources and opportunities (i.e., entrepreneurial adventures, pursuit of higher education, etc.) that may not be afforded in other countries around the world. The United States, however, has not only been blessed for its financial resources and opportunities. We have been blessed with many other resources such as opportunities to invest in ourselves by growing and becoming the most authentic person we can be (i.e., spiritually, socially, emotionally, psychologically, physically, etc.), in other words, the investment in bettering yourself, the healthy self. There have been numerous published articles and books on self-improvement, love, relationships, singleness, marriage, and divorce. In addition, we have attended so many marriage conferences, seminars, and retreats that we should be experts by now in terms of modeling healthy and functional marriages. Sadly, why isn't this the case?

In reality, it seems that individuals are experiencing difficulties with achieving and maintaining healthy marriages. This takes me back to my premise. If we have been blessed with an abundance of information on the aforementioned topics, then why does the rate of divorce continue to impact Christians? This issue is of great concern for not only me, but other individuals whom I have spent countless hours engaging and dialoguing on this very topic. What is the problem? one may ask. We have discussed ideas from individuals settling for less than God's best (choosing not to wait on God out of sheer desperation and/or anxiety, the biological-clock-is-ticking syndrome, etc.) to compromising God's standards, to growing restless and weary in your time of waiting, and so forth.

There Is Hope

We know this to be an issue, but what is the solution? you may ask. I will discuss in more detail in the subsequent chapters. Albeit, I believe a new day has come where God wants to do something different in the heart of every single man and woman, providing we will allow Him to do the work that will produce something different. Even though He loves us enough to give us free will to make choices, I believe God still wants us to make choices according to His perfect will that will be healthy and beneficial for us. I remember in my early days of graduate study at Azusa Pacific University, I took a course on psychological theories in counseling. One of the theories that I studied was a theory by the name of solution focused therapy (SFT). SFT's central philosophy was centered on three main tenets:

1. If it's not broken, don't fix it.
2. If it's working, do more of it.
3. If it's not working, do something different (Murdock, 2009).

With this being said, I propose that it is time for us Christians to do something different. Our pursuit of love has become problematic, and it is discouraging to hear stories of individuals we know that have dissolved their marriage. It is time for singles across the United States and even across the world to make some changes, to do something different. You have been made aware of the statistics regarding the rate of divorce for Christians. Let's face the hard truth. It is time for Christian men and women who are single to make changes in terms of how we approach the subject of finding the one, how we approach finding love.

Conclusion

I have had many conversations with family members, girlfriends, guy friends, couples (married or divorce), and they oftentimes ask or wonder why I am not married. I like to say to them, with a big ole' smile on my face, "Marriage is not like buying a cute designer purse or a fierce pair of shoes." After buying, if you decide that you do not like the purse or the pair of shoes, you can simply return the items to the store. In terms of a finding the one, once married, you cannot return the individual should you decide or realize that you are not happy with the individual. Therefore, my response to the above question is that I am choosing to wait on God. In the words of one pastor, waiting on God may take a little longer, but it will be right when he's done with you and the individual he has for you. I like this saying because I have resolved in my mind that I won't—in fact, I refuse to—marry just anyone for the sake of saying I have somebody or because I got tired of waiting. I have purposed in my heart to wait on God. Let me just tell you that I have found, the longer you learn to wait, the easier it becomes to wait. I find myself telling people, "I don't mind waiting, whether standing in line or waiting for some type of service. I'm getting good at it." Perhaps, you need to get "good at waiting." And let me also tell you there is hope. This topic of waiting leads me to my next chapter, which addresses the question, what's wrong with waiting? I believe this is one of the solutions to minimizing the rate of divorce among Christians. I hope the next chapter blesses you!

CHAPTER 3

What's Wrong with Waiting?

"I wait for the Lord, my soul waits, and in
his word I put my hope. My soul waits for the
Lord more than watchmen wait for the morning,
more than watchmen wait for the morning."

—Psalms 130:5–6 (KJV)

One day, I was grading a stack of papers, and I came across words written by one of my students. The words caught my attention. It was a statement regarding wisdom, which is a topic that I like to read and discuss with anyone interested. The statement read, "By three methods we may learn wisdom: first by reflection, which is the noblest; second, by imitation, which is easiest; and third by experience, which is the most bitter" (Confucius). My heart began to beat rapidly. The latter portion of the statement struck me. I thought of the proverb that states, "Each heart knows its own bitterness, and no one else can share its joy" (Proverbs 14:10, NIV). You see, I am all too familiar with the third part of the Confucius's statement, wisdom obtained by bitter experiences or, to some, known as the school of hard knocks. As a result of bitter experiences, I value wisdom very much. The entire book of Proverbs is basically a book about obtaining wisdom. In fact, the first four chapters of the book of Proverbs addressed the topic of wisdom in great detail, from warning against rejecting wisdom to moral benefits of embracing wisdom. In Proverbs 4:7, the writer, believed to be Solomon, stated, "Wisdom is supreme; therefore get wisdom. Though it costs all you have, get understanding" (NIV). I have found that if you allow, wisdom will keep you. For the most part, if you listen, wisdom will keep you from suffering heartaches and disappointments that you do not necessarily have to experience in the bitter or hard way.

Moreover, I believe obtaining wisdom and waiting on God are synonymous. Like Confucius's statement, which states that one of the ways one can acquire wisdom is through bitter experiences, I submit that one does not have to acquire wisdom by bitter experiences. Think about the following phraseologies, of which I am sure you are acquainted: "If I had to do over again," "If I knew what I know now, then, I would have," "Hindsight is twenty-twenty," "School of hard knocks," and so on. These are all familiar colloquialisms, and one thing that they seem to have in common is the theme of regret. One way to acquire wisdom is simply by waiting on God. In essence, I am saying it is wise to wait on God. There is much to be learned and much insight to be gained when we trust God in whatever journey we find ourselves in. Part of our journey may involve just waiting on God and trusting him for his timing. His word states that he makes all things beautiful in his timing (Ecclesiastes 3:11). We do not always have to learn wisdom the hard way. We will reap far more benefits when we wait on God, hear his voice, and do what he has said—nothing more, nothing less. We get ourselves in trouble and create a mess when we do not choose to wait on God. We take the risk of learning or obtaining wisdom the hard way or, should I say, bitterly. It is my hope that as I share my experiences of waiting on God, times of frustrations, confusion, and what seemed like setbacks or delays, that you learn the wisdom I gained through the waiting process. If we listen to wisdom when she speaks, unlike Confucius's statement, obtaining wisdom does not have to be acquired through bitter experiences. I charge you, "he who has ears, let him hear" (Matthew 11:15, NIV) what the spirit of the Lord may be saying.

Waiting Is Good

Let me begin this section by discussing an interesting trend that is beginning to gain momentum. This particular trend appeared to begin in the twentieth century and continued into the twenty-first century. The trend depicts men and women marrying for the first time at a later age. The data was based on the 2006–2010 National Survey of Family Growth (NSFG), utilizing a national representative sample of 12,279 women and 10,403 men (ages 15–44) in the United States. The results found that the median age for first marriage was 25.8 for women and 28.3 for men. In addition, the US Census Bureau (as cited in Yen, 2011) reported a decline in women marrying in their teens and men postponing marriages past their college-age years. According to Yen (2011), a reporter from the Huffington Post cites statistics based on the 2009 US census for men and women marrying at a later age:

"For instance, in 1970, more than half of men, 57 percent, were between the ages of 20 and 24 when they first married. By 2009, the age distribution was much wider, with 24 percent marrying between the ages of 20 and 24, 34 percent marrying between the ages of 25 and 29, 20 percent marrying between the ages of 30 and 34, and 9 percent marrying between the ages of 35 and 39 (para. 12). Similarly for women, in 1970, 42 percent of women were teens when they married, and by the age of 24 about 88 percent of women had a first marriage. By 2009, the shares had dropped to 7 percent and 38 percent respectively (para. 13). As a whole, since 1970, the median age at first marriage increased from 22.5 years to 28.4 for men and from 20.6 years to 26.5 for women (para 14.). Yen concluded that younger people may be delaying marriage as they struggle to find work, therefore resisting long-term commitments."

Interesting trend, right? Let me ask you this question. When you hear the word *waiting*, what thoughts come to mind? If you are like most people, it is a word that is not readily embraced or does not necessarily evoke a positive emotion or response. Why do you suppose this is the case? I think one reason is that we have been conditioned by the messages of our modern-day culture. We want what we want now, and we want it fast! You've already heard the vernacular: we live in an immediate gratification or microwaveable society. The message is pretty clear. No one wants to wait for anything; it's an inconvenience to wait. However, if you have been walking with God for any length of time, you know He does not think this way. There is nothing instant or immediate about God. He favors the journey and the waiting process that time brings. In addition, he does not allow us (his children) to get away with this type of thinking or mentality. God sees waiting as good, and there are many valuable fruits of wisdom to be learned in seasons of waiting. God simply uses the time we have to wait to refine, strengthen, mature, and purify us so that we can be healthy (spirit, soul, and body) enough to receive the promise when it comes. But when we choose not to wait on God and rush the process, we give birth to Ishmaels (born of the flesh, Genesis 15–16). You cannot fool God. He is not mocked. "A man reaps what he sows. The one who sows to please his sinful nature, from that nature will reap destruction. The one who sows to please the Spirit, from the

Spirit will reap eternal life" (Galatians 6:7–8, NIV). What are you sowing? If you are sowing to the Spirit, great! Keep doing so, for at the proper time you will reap a harvest if you do not give up (v. 9). If you are sowing to the flesh, I exhort you. Give up the plans. It may look good on the outside (1 Samuel 16:7) and feel good on the inside; however, in the long run, that which you sowed in the flesh will eventually catch up. Again, God is not mocked. You may be able to fool others, but not God. It is better to wait on God for the promises. Waiting is good, and hope does not disappoint (Romans 5:5). Waiting on God may not be the easiest to do, but we can choose how we wait. We can wait with joy and enjoy the journey on the way to the promise, or we can become disgruntled or impatient, thereby causing the waiting process to take longer than necessary. Ask the nation of Israel.

What Are You Waiting On?

How much time do you think you spend waiting? You probably have not thought about the amount of time you spend waiting in a day, week, a month, or a year, for that matter. In reality, we spend an exuberant amount of time waiting. I came across an article called "Why Waiting Is Torture." The author stated that Americans spend about 37 billion hours each year waiting in lines (Stone, 2012). That's a good chunk of time spent waiting. Not only do we wait in lines, we also wait in other aspects of our lives such as waiting to be served in restaurants, waiting in traffic, waiting in airports, waiting at doctors' appointments (House, 2012), and so on. Starting to get my point? Therefore, I ask you specifically, as you read this chapter, what are you waiting on? Could you be waiting for Mr. or Mrs. Right? How long do you think you will have to wait, thirty-seven billion hours? For some it may feel like that long; however, let's hope it does not take any longer than necessary.

Let's face it. Waiting is a necessary part of life, and we cannot escape its confines. What does it means to wait, or rather, what does it mean when we wait on God? According to Merriam-Webster's Online Dictionary (2012), *wait* means to stay in place in expectation of, to look forward expectantly. Similarly, Dictionary.com (2011) defines *wait* in terms of remaining inactive until a specified time or until an event occurs, to be ready. Would you say these are good definitions? I would say so; however, waiting on God does not necessarily imply that our time of waiting is inactive. When we wait on God, we are in a sense inactive or at rest (meaning we are not trying to help God out or help God bring the promise to pass by working in the flesh). We should be at rest or inactive in our works; however, our faith should be active. In fact, Paul, through the inspiration of the Holy Spirit, said "without faith, it is impossible to please God" (Hebrews 11:6, NIV). God responds to faith, and our active faith causes him to move on our behalf.

Nevertheless, most of us do not embrace waiting, seasons of waiting, or times of waiting. We become impatient, cynical, and restless. Some of us just give up and compromise; others walk away from God altogether. If we are honest, we would admit that waiting on God is not easy. Know anyone like this? We know many stories in the Bible of individuals who have waited on God and received the promise.

King David Waited

Remember King David? God chose David to be the next king of Israel because he had rejected Saul as king of Israel (1 Samuel 15). God instructed the prophet Samuel to go to the house of

Jesse and anoint one of his sons. In short, out of all Jesse's sons, God chose the youngest, David. He was the one to be anointed king over Israel (1 Samuel 16:1–13). However, it would be years after King Saul's death before he would assume the throne. Even though Saul was still the king of Israel, the spirit of the Lord had departed from him. In David's time of waiting, he served as Saul's armor-bearer (1 Samuel 16:14–23), fought many battles on behalf of Israel, and endured much opposition. Some of the opposition was at the hands of King Saul, who sought to kill him out of jealousy. After the death of Saul, David was anointed (a second time) king over the house of Judah in Hebron (2 Samuel 2:1–30). David eventually (years later) assumed his position as king over Israel. Get it? God chose David to be king over Israel, but it was not an overnight process. In the end, King David reigned for forty years over Israel, seven years in Hebron and thirty-three years in Jerusalem (1 Kings 2:10–12).

Abraham and Sarah Waited

What about the classic story of Abraham and Sarah? This story never stops blessing me. Truly, with God all things are possible. I like to think of the story of Abraham and Sarah as the cornerstone of what faith looks like. We learn from Abraham what it means to purely have faith. You know the story. God promised Abraham and Sarah that a son would be born to them from their own bodies. Of course, they messed up, and as a result Ishmael (mother was Hagar, Sarah's maidservant, and father was Abraham) was born (Genesis 16). Nevertheless, Abraham and Sarah's unbelief did not nullify what God had told Abraham in Genesis 15:4. God meant what he said when he told Abraham that a son coming from his own body would be his heir. Abraham and Sarah, who were past the childbearing age, waited twenty-five years for the promise to come to pass (Genesis 15:4, 17:16–19, 18:10–15, 21:1–5). Despite some unbelief, God still credited Abraham as the father of faith (Hebrews 11:11). Now, do not panic. I am not saying you have to wait twenty-five years for your promise to come to pass. The point of sharing this story is that despite some impatience and unbelief, Abraham and Sarah still had to wait on the promise God was referring (Genesis 17:17–18), and God honored his word indeed (Genesis 21).

Joseph Waited

What about the story of Joseph and his coat of many rich colors? This famous coat was a coat given by his father, Jacob (Genesis 37:3–4), and this coat was a source of tension between Joseph and his brothers. His brothers saw that Jacob loved Joseph more than any of them. This difference is what fueled the hatred for Joseph by his brothers. To make matters worse, God gave Joseph two dreams (Genesis 37:1–11). In the first dream, his brothers' sheaves gathered around Joseph's sheaves and bowed down to Joseph's sheaves. In the second dream, the sun, moon, and eleven stars (representing the tribes of Jacob, later renamed Israel) bowed down to Joseph. After his brothers heard the dreams, they hated Joseph even more. However, Joseph's father, Jacob (Israel), kept the dreams in mind, but the dreams would not come to pass until years later. One day Joseph went out to check on his brothers (at his father's insistence). Joseph's brothers saw him coming in a distance. They plotted and conspired to kill him, but ended up selling him into slavery for twenty shekels of silver (Genesis 37:28). He was sold to the Ishmaelites, who took him to Egypt (Genesis 37:19–28). Joseph was bought by Potiphar, the captain of the guard for

Pharaoh. Eventually, Joseph found favor with Potiphar, and he was put in charge of his entire household. Later, trouble would follow, as Potiphar's wife became attracted to Joseph. One day, she wanted him to sleep with her, and Joseph turned her down; in fact, he fled the room. Potiphar's wife became enraged and falsely accused him of violating her (Genesis 39). Joseph was put in prison; however, God was with him. He won the favor of the prison warden, and Joseph was put in charge of all the prisoners (Genesis 39:20–23). Years passed while Joseph was in prison until a divine opportunity came for him to interpret Pharaoh's two dreams. Joseph was not only a dreamer, but also had the ability to interpret dreams. Joseph interpreted Pharaoh's dreams, which revealed seven years of fruitfulness and seven years of famine. Pharaoh was so pleased with Joseph that he placed him second in command to him (Genesis 41:1–43).

The dreams that God gave Joseph when he was seventeen years old (Genesis 37) would not come to pass for thirteen years; Joseph was thirty years old when the plan of God began to unfold. Joseph waited on God and as a result became second in command to Pharaoh (Genesis 41:46). Joseph was an administrator over the entire land of Egypt. After many years of being separated from his father and brothers, Joseph revealed himself to his brothers, who had come to Egypt for food due to famine in their land, Canaan (Genesis 42–45). Joseph would have had the right to respond in anger and bitterness, but he did not. He responded the opposite because he realized that what the brothers meant for evil, God meant it for good (Genesis 50:19). It was for the saving of lives that God sent Joseph ahead of his family and his people. God used Joseph's position in Egypt to preserve a remnant (nation of Israel) on earth and to save his family's lives by a great deliverance (Genesis 45:4–7). Joseph waited thirteen years to see God's dreams come full circle.

WHAT'S WRONG WITH WAITING?

Queen Esther Waited

Then, there was Hadassah (her Jewish name) or Esther (her Persian name), who was the cousin of Mordecai. Esther was not born into royalty nor was she born of noble descent. Esther became queen as a result of someone else's rebellion and disrespect. Long story short, Queen Vashti refused to attend her husband's (King Xerxes) banquet. This rebellion and disrespect on Queen Vashti's behalf cost her the crown. As a result of this rebellion and disrespect, a royal edict was issued into the laws of Persia and Media that Queen Vashti would never again enter the presence of the king. In addition, a new edict was issued, which stated that her royal position be given to someone other than her (Esther 1:1–22).

After King Xerxes's anger subsided, he seemed to regret the edict that was issued on behalf of Queen Vashti, which could not be repealed. It was suggested by his personal attendants that a search be made for beautiful young virgins for the king. The girl who pleased the king would be queen instead of Vashti. As a result of this search, many young girls were brought to the citadel of Susa and placed in the care of Hegai. Esther was one of the young virgins taken to the king's palace and entrusted to Hegai, the king's eunuch. During their time of waiting to go in to see the king, each virgin received beauty treatments. Out of all the virgins, Esther pleased and won the favor of Hegai and was immediately provided with beauty treatments and special food. In addition, she was assigned seven maids, and her quarters were moved into the best place in the harem. Before each virgin went in to see the king, they had to complete twelve months of beauty treatments, six months with oil of myrrh and six with perfumes and costumes. When it came time for Esther to go to the king, she took nothing other than what Hegai suggested. Esther won the favor of everyone who saw her. When the king saw her, he was attracted to her more than any of the other virgins and she won his favor and approval. The king set a royal crown on her head and made her queen instead of Vashti (Esther 2:1–18).

I am not sure how long Esther waited overall, as there were probably other virgins that went before her to see the king. One thing we know for sure, that each virgin had to undergo one year of preparation before they were allowed to see the king. And even though Esther would later be chosen by the king as the new queen, she was no exception. She still had to wait out her one year of preparation. What I learned about the story of Esther was that it was a process before she became queen. She was not queen overnight. She had to humble herself and surrender to the process if she wanted her chance meeting with the king. God allowed the process of time to prepare Esther. When she was ready, her time came, and we know the outcome!

Ruth Waited

Lastly, we all know the sad story of Ruth; her husband dies. However, the story does not end sad. Ruth was left with a choice, go back to her mother's household (Ruth 1:8–9) or follow her mother-in-law (Naomi) to a strange place that she had never known. The word of God states that Ruth clung to Naomi and would not say good-bye (Ruth 1:14). Ruth told Naomi, "Where you go I go, where you stay I stay. Your people will be my people and your God my God" (Ruth 1:16, NIV). Naomi and Ruth set out to go back to Naomi's hometown, Bethlehem. Naomi had a relative on her husband's (who was also dead) side. He was Boaz, a man of standing from the clan of Elimelech. Ruth began to glean in his fields and would pick up what was left behind by the harvesters. One day Boaz came

WHAT'S WRONG WITH WAITING?

to his field and greeted the harvesters. He noticed Ruth and asked his foreman, "Whose young woman is that" (Ruth 2:1–5, NIV)? The foreman told him what he knew about Ruth, what she had done for her mother-in-law (Naomi), how she left her mother and father's homeland and came with her mother-in-law to live with a people she did not know before. From that day on, Ruth found favor in the eyes of Boaz. He allowed her to glean in his field as much as she wanted.

One day Naomi, Ruth's mother-in-law, stated, "should I not try and find a home for you, where you will be provided for? Is not Boaz, with whose servant girl you have been, a kinsman of ours" (Ruth 3:1–2, NIV)? Naomi gave Ruth instructions, which consisted of where Boaz will be and how she should present herself to him. Ruth, per Naomi's instructions, washed, perfumed herself, and put on her best clothes. Later on, Ruth went to the threshing floor, where Boaz was working late that night. Per Naomi's instructions, she did not let him know she was there until after he had finished eating and drinking. After Boaz went to lie down, Ruth went over to uncover his feet and lie down. Per Naomi's instructions, Boaz would tell her what to do next (Ruth 3:3–4). Boaz realized a woman was lying at his feet. Ruth identified herself as his servant and said to spread the corner of his garment over her since he was a kinsman redeemer (Ruth 3:5–9). Even though Boaz was a kinsman redeemer, he told Ruth there was one closer than him. Boaz told Ruth to stay for the night, and in the morning, if this kinsman redeemer wanted to redeem, good; if not, he would do it. Ruth lay at his feet until morning and got up before anyone saw her. Boaz blessed her before she left by pouring into the shawl she was wearing six measures of barley. He instructed her to not let anyone know that a woman came to the threshing floor. Ruth went back to Naomi and told her everything that happened. Then Naomi said, "Wait, my daughter, until you find out what happens. For the man will not rest until the matter is settled today" (Ruth 3:10–18, NIV). Boaz kept his word. He found the closet kinsman redeemer. However, he could not redeem because his own estate would be endangered. Therefore, he asked Boaz to redeem. For the transfer of the property to become legal in earlier times in Israel, one party took off his sandal and gave it to the other; the kinsman redeemer gave his sandal to Boaz. Boaz announced to the elders and witnesses that he had bought from Naomi all the property of Elimelech (Naomi's husband), Kilion, and Mahlon (Naomi's sons). Naomi's husband and two sons had died in Moab, which led her and Ruth to travel back to her homeland in Bethlehem. As a result of Boaz's purchase of Naomi's property, he also acquired Mahlon's widow, Ruth, as his wife (in order to maintain the name of the dead with his property so that his name would not disappear from among the family and the town records) (Ruth 4:1–12). Boaz and Ruth later had a son and called him Obed. He was the father of Jesse. Jesse was the father of David; that is King David (mentioned earlier in this chapter).

Conclusion

I could share more stories about how individuals in the Bible trusted God and waited on Him to bring the promise to pass in their life. Some will tell you that it seems as if waiting on God to bring the right mate in your life is downright difficult. The waiting process tests your character and faith. Little does a person know that the process of waiting on God is purposeful for building character and pruning areas in your life that need to be addressed before that mate comes. I hear teachers and pastors say, to marry the right person, you need to be the right person. What does that mean? The answer to that question lies in the process of waiting on God. For some of us the journey to the altar will be smooth sailing while for others arduous and uncertain. Nevertheless, we all have to put in our time of waiting. I cannot tell you how long you will have to wait. For some the wait may not be long, and for others it may seem like an eternity. "He who promised is faithful" (Hebrews 10:23, NIV). When you choose to wait on God, He will honor your time of waiting and bless you immensely beyond what you can think or imagine (Ephesians 3:20), and his blessings will bring no sorrow (Proverbs 10:22).

CHAPTER 4

There Is Purpose in Waiting

"And hope does not disappoint…"

—Romans 5:5 (NIV)

I hope that you were encouraged by the stories in chapter 3 of the individuals of the Bible that waited on God. You might as well face it and get comfortable with waiting. We will all spend our lives waiting on something or someone. We will never cease from waiting. I can tell you that the times I waited on God were times of hope, joy, and expectancy. However, there were also some times of pain, confusion, anxiety, and fear. It was in these times of waiting that my relationship with the Lord grew stronger and closer. I came to know him as a friend, a father, and my husband. Women and men, until your relationship with the Lord becomes solid and fulfilling, your wait for your future spouse may take longer than you planned or desired. God is a jealous God, and he will not have any person, place, or thing before him. Unbeknownst to me, my season of waiting was to purge these things from my life and place them in their proper order. In this chapter, I want to share my experiences of how God used the process of time to teach me about waiting. I had learned to wait with contentment. However, this was not always the case. I sometimes jokingly tell people when they apologize for taking longer than expected, "It's okay. I am good at waiting." I usually get laughs, but internally, I really mean what I say. I am not at all bothered by the fact that I have to wait. Just like individuals you read about in chapter 3 had to learn to wait on God, I too had to learn to wait!

As I stated before, I will share three experiences that forever shaped my life, causing me to grow and mature. These experiences taught me something not only about waiting on God, but the love of God. The time I spent waiting in these three experiences was very painful, filled with frustrations, wrestling moments with God, disappointments, and discouragement. I did experience some days of peace, joy, and victories. However, these days seemed short-lived in comparison to the dark days I experienced. Nevertheless, these experiences brought me to a place of intimacy with God. It is a place where I know him and know his voice. This place is the secret place. There is a place in my heart that God has captured; not even my future husband will be able to reside in this place. I will begin with my first story.

Three Times the Charm

On December 18, 1998, I had finished my master's in clinical psychology with an emphasis in the marriage and family licensing track (MFT) from Azusa Pacific University. After graduate school, I began working full time, but did not apply to become a registered MFT intern until several years later. In all honesty, I was not sure if I wanted to pursue the licensure track. I remember feeling burnt out during my traineeship, and because of the burnout, I did not think becoming a therapist was the right fit for me. I thought I could do well with just my master's degree. Nevertheless, God changed my heart several years later, and I decided to pursue becoming a licensed MFT. Once I got serious, I completed the application packet to register as a California MFT intern so that I could accumulate the rest of my hours towards licensure. After finishing the application packet, I had a moment of doubt before I would mail the application materials to the California Board of Behavioral Sciences. I remember one morning looking at the packet, and I heard the Holy Spirit tell me to mail the packet, and so I did. I was blessed with employment that would pay me a salary plus benefits. Additionally, my employer would also provide the supervision that I needed to accumulate the rest of the hours I needed in order to be eligible for the California state licensing MFT exams. I needed a total of three thousand hours in order to be eligible to take the two MFT state exams.

In 2006, I had begun the process of taking the state exams. I had passed the first state exam on the first attempt. I was excited, elated, and felt confident about the second exam. I just knew I would pass. To my dismay, passing the second exam would be a challenge. Each time you do not pass the exam, you have to wait six months in order to be eligible to take the exam again. It took me three times to pass the second exam. The first time I took the second exam, I missed the passing score by one point. I was sick to my stomach and disappointed for days. I could not believe I was so close. I said to my mom, "Why couldn't they just have given it to me?" The second attempt left me feeling even more discouraged. Truth be told, I should have rescheduled the exam because I had just gotten over the flu, and my head was not as clear on that day. Needless to say, I did not pass the exam and missed the passing score by six points. At that point, I was not sure if I would continue in the process towards licensure since I failed and had been disappointed. I took a break from studying the second exam altogether. I waited several months before I got up the strength and motivation to take the exam again.

They say third time is the charm because on March 12, 2008, I passed the second exam. I was now a California licensed marriage and family therapist. I was excited as I left the examination room. The examiner was excited for me and celebrated with me (I guess she had never seen a person jumping up and down before) and encouraged me as I went on my way to share the news with others. Overall, it took me one and a half years to become licensed. As I reflect back on the journey, accumulating the hours toward licensure was relatively smooth; however, the journey towards passing the state exams did not prove to be as smooth. The scripture that comes to mind is Proverbs 24:10, "If thou faint in the day of adversity, thy strength is small" (KJV). I did not realize that God was beginning to teach me something about the process of waiting. Waiting on God builds strength, persistence, and character.

The Refining Process Continues

My next journey began as God had been impressing upon my heart to return to school to obtain a PhD. I did not want to as I was completely satisfied with my master's degree. After some gentle prodding from the Lord and encouragement from a former supervisor, I finally relented. In June, the summer month, of 2006, I started my first quarter at Walden University studying psychology (with an emphasis in the teaching track). The coursework was a breeze. I had fun and learned a great deal. After two and a half years, I had completed all coursework, and it was time for me to begin the dissertation phrase. I was quite excited and optimistic to be at this point in finishing my PhD. I set a goal to finish my dissertation in five quarters. I thought it would be a breeze, just like my coursework had been a breeze. Little did I know, I was being set up for another life-shaping experience.

I began the dissertation process in the summer, June 2008. (I had just completed the MFT licensing process several months prior.) The first dissertation quarter went smoothly, as I was right on track in terms of the progress that I wanted to make. After the first quarter, I experienced less smooth days. I was in for a rude awakening. My writing and research skills underwent much critique and scrutiny by my dissertation committee members. Before the dissertation process, I thought I had pretty good writing and researching skills. I mean, after all, had I not already been demonstrating these skills and proving myself in my coursework? Nevertheless, the critique was so intense that I was beginning to take their feedback personal. For many days, I saw numerous red marks, deletions, and insertions. I began to experience feelings of rejection by this scientific process of academic hazing, as I like to call it. I also began to experience feelings of low self-esteem, low confidence (of course, I had already struggled with these issues, and the dissertation process did not make my issues any better), and feeling less than intelligent compared to some of my counterparts who were breezing through the process. There were countless revisions (I stopped keeping track) and hours I spent writing, rewriting, and researching. Slowly, I realized, the goal that I had set to complete my dissertation in five quarters was not going to be as easy as I had originally thought. In my time of waiting and desiring for this process to be over, I experienced some very dark days. I felt so sad at times, discouraged, and even angry, angry with the individuals that seemingly were holding me back from completing in the time frame I had envisioned. I spent a lot of time crying and praying. I never cried and prayed so much. I remember a time (after getting another round of revisions) I went to seek

God, and I said to him with tears and feelings of pressure and weight on my shoulders, "I am going to quit. I don't need a doctorate. You were the one that wanted me to go back to school. I was content with my master's degree." Then, not expecting God to respond to me immediately, I heard a quiet voice say, "What is this I am hearing about you quitting? You can do all things through me, who will give you the strength." Needless to say, I pondered on these words in silence. The tears dried from my eyes, and I got up from my knees and came out of the closet I was in and pressed forward (Philippians 3:14), until the next time of being frustrated, sad, and once again in tears.

Truth be told, even though I got a clear word from God that he would give me the strength to finish, I still wrestled with my ability to finish this dissertation process and finished well. Each time, I had to lay down the burden, the stress, the anxiety, the anger, and the discouragement. I remember crying and throwing myself on the couch (like a two-year-old's tantrum) after I had received what I considered at the time negative feedback from members on my dissertation committee. In retrospect, the feedback was constructive, designed to make me a better writer, researcher, and produce good work. Nevertheless, this tantrum-like behavior would happen often. I wanted to be done and over this process, and I was starting to see the members of my dissertation committee as enemies. However, in time, I began to see that after each constructive feedback from my committee members, I noticed that I would not cry as much or engage in the tantrum episodes. I noticed that I was standing, getting a little stronger, and receiving the feedback comments without becoming weary and frustrated. My thinking and response to the feedback had changed. I began to see my dissertation committee as individuals who were trying to help me. They were not against me or were trying to hold me back. They were not trying to make my life miserable. I mean, they have been on numerous committees. Surely they must know what they were doing by now! They just wanted me to produce the best work possible. One day my dissertation chair said to me, "Good work takes time." In retrospect, I could see what she meant. In time, my perspective changed about the dissertation process, and I became strengthened as a result.

It finally took me two and half years to finish my dissertation, a far cry from the five quarters (one year and three months) that I had initially planned. My dissertation was approved and conferred on November 11, 2010. I was excited to get the final e-mail from the chief academic officer who had approved my dissertation. I walked in the winter ceremony on January 23, 2011, in Miami, Florida. There were numerous things I learned in this journey. For one, I saw myself changed, and God used this dissertation process to do that work in me. I was becoming solid in the Lord (Psalm 105:37). God was establishing me (1 Peter 5:10). I also learned in this journey that life on this fallen earth was never designed to be easy. Life is about conflict, pressure, and challenges. I learned it is how we cope and respond to the conflict, pressure, and challenges that can make all the difference. I once heard a pastor and author say we have to learn to act (responding in action) and not react (blowing up emotionally). I had spent some of the time during the dissertation process reacting. However, by the time God was done with me, I was no longer reacting, but acting. Since we cannot avoid waiting, how we cope and respond in our seasons of waiting can make our quality of life so much more enjoyable and easier. In fact, James, through the inspiration of the Holy Spirit, said "Consider it pure joy my brothers, whenever you face trials of many kinds, because you know that the testing of your faith develops perseverance. Perseverance must finish its work so that you may be mature and complete. Not lacking anything" (James, 1:2–4, NIV). God was using this dissertation process to refine, strengthen, mature, and perfect me (Psalms 138:8). I celebrated with family and friends that this part of my life was finally over. Little did I know, I was about to experience another process of strengthening and refining.

Love at Last?

During my PhD journey, I was standing in faith and waiting on God for a husband. I had a strong desire to get married and start a family. I had been praying for my future husband around the age of twenty-four. I thought my husband would come soon. As stated previously, I am now forty-five years old. I discovered that my idea of soon was not the same as God's idea of soon. With God a day is like a thousand years and a thousand years is like a day (Psalms 90:4 and 2 Peter 3:8). In my naiveté, I did not think I would have to wait very long for him to find me. I thought I was mature and ready to receive. As the years rolled by and seeing girlfriends get married and start a family, I began to realize that my prayers for marriage were not going to be answered so quickly. I was going to have to wait longer than I wanted and expected. In my time of waiting on God, I wrestled with so many emotions. I was angry, frustrated, sad, and confused, sometimes with God and sometimes at the men (including my father) that hurt me by disappointing me. There were mountaintop experiences and valley moments. Once again, the valley moments came more frequent than the mountaintop experiences. I had dated emotionally and/or spiritually immature men, who had unresolved issues or unhealthy boundaries with ex-girlfriends from their past, men who had unresolved issues with their fathers, who did not have job stability or a career. These men seemed confused and fickle and had some type of abuse, abandonment, and/or rejection issue. I know that was a mouthful, but my time of waiting on God for my husband allowed me to see the patterns in which all of my ex-boyfriends shared. I wrestled with trusting men and wondered if there were any safe men in the church. I had opened my heart only for it to be broken, mistreated, and taken for granted. I wrestled with the feelings that God would not do it for me. He was willing to do it for others, but not me. I wrestled with feelings of not being worthy of marriage, of being a wife and a mother. Why did my ex-boyfriends discard me so easily? Why was I not worth fighting for? Wasn't I a keeper? I never felt so low and bad about myself. I felt rejected and wrestled with resentment, unforgiveness, and anger—all supporting spirits of the principality of bitterness (Art Mathias). One morning, on January 7, 2009, as I was waking up, I heard Proverbs 24:27, which states, "Finish your outdoor work and get your fields ready, after that, build your house(NIV). I knew what God was saying to me. I was to focus (at that time) finish my PhD, get settled in the career/ministry he was calling me to pursue, and then the time for marriage and family would come.

Importance of Waiting

To God, waiting is good, never wasteful, and purposeful. If we can adopt this attitude, you will see that waiting on God yields many benefits. I remember my former church opened the doors (May 20–July 8, 2011) for anyone wanting to come to seek the Lord for direction in their life. On the first night of seeking the Lord, I felt impressed about the word suffering. In this time, several scriptures came to me. In 1 Peter 5:10 (NIV), it states "that after you have suffered a little while, God will himself restore you and make you strong, firm, and steadfast." Sometimes knowing God's will for your life may produce suffering, especially when what God is showing you in the spirit does not look like what you see in the natural. Suffering will make you strong, firm, and steadfast. In Romans 5:3–5, we are commanded by Paul to rejoice in our sufferings (if that were possible) "knowing that our suffering produces perseverance; perseverance, character; and character, hope"(NIV). As I read and meditated on this passage, I thought, "Lord, is that what you have been doing in me this whole time of waiting?" I saw waiting on the Lord as a time of suffering. Another passage came to me, Hebrews 12:11, which states "discipline is painful, later on it produces a harvest of righteousness and peace for those who have been trained by it"(NIV). In James 1:2–4, we are commanded by James to count it all joy when we face trials of many kinds. Why? because "the testing of our faith develops perseverance. Perseverance must finish its work so that you may be mature and complete, not lacking anything" (NIV). As I sat in the sanctuary and meditated on these passages, I began to realize the work the Lord was been doing in me all this time.

One morning while I was attending a local church where I lived at the time, listening to the pastor teach out of John 13:7, certain words jumped out to me. I knew the Lord was talking to me. Jesus was washing the disciples' feet, and Simon Peter questioned his act. Jesus said, "You do not realize now what I am doing, but later you will understand"(NIV). Even though Jesus was talking about much more than clean feet, I felt like that day God was washing his word with my heart by bringing me revelation and some light into my circumstance with all three of my experiences. In all of the aforementioned experiences, I can look back over them and say that I understood that I needed to go through them simply because of the fruit that came as a result. Though I did not understand at that time what God was doing, I can see more clearly now. However, I will tell you that through the valley moments, pain, suffering, and my time of waiting on God, I can see what the process produced according to Romans 5:3–5, 1 Peter 5:10, and Hebrews 12:11:

- Strength
- Firmness
- Steadfastness (Patience)
- Perseverance
- Character
- Hope
- Harvest of righteousness
- Peace
- Maturity
- Completeness/Wholeness

Therefore, I exhort you, whatever you are waiting on God for, know that you will reap many benefits if you succumb to the refining process. Do not take the easy way out or settle for less than God's perfect will. Do not give up or throw in the towel. But let God have his way with you. If he asks for it, give it to him. Lay yourself on that surgical table and allow him to remove anything that will keep you from being the best he intended and created you to be. If he removes it, he is more than capable of closing the incision and healing the wound. Allow him to perfect you through whatever circumstance he chooses to allow in the perfecting process. It may feel painful, uncomfortable, and unbearable. Remember, God is on your side. He is not trying to throw you under the bus, and he certainly does not get pleasure out of our pain and suffering. However, like any good parent, if he sees an area that will become a stumbling block or hinder you in anyway, he will target it and ask you to surrender it for your ultimate good. If you are experiencing this right now, remember there is healing in his wings (Malachi 4:2). This too shall pass. I end this chapter with an excerpt from one of my journal entries as I reflect on this journey of waiting. I simply titled it "Emotions:"

THERE IS PURPOSE IN WAITING

Waiting on the promises of God has taken me through a myriad of emotions. I have felt such intense feelings of sadness, anger, hopelessness, discouragement, confusion, indifference, fear, doubting, and shock. Various experiences along this journey have evoked these emotions more than once—sometimes one or more of them at the same time. God was so gracious and faithful to bring me through each moment. I do not know how he does it. In his awesomeness, he holds you up and doesn't let you fall, doesn't let you go. It took me some time to get to this place of faith and for me to actually rest in the promises of God over my life. I now know what it means to rest. It means you do need to strive or need a lot of convincing. It is a confidence and peace that God said it, that settles it, and he will always do what he said he will do. It took time for me to get to the place of walking in the supernatural, on water, being comfortable in it and not freaking out or reacting in my flesh. Walking on water is uncomfortable. There is no support to the flesh, none whatsoever. Maybe time is what he (referring to the man I thought was my husband at that time) needs for God to do the work in him like he did in me—time to see, hear, and mature. I do not know what the gift of time will bring, but I do know already from two witnesses that said to me I am going to be glad that I waited that I will be looking at him saying, "Lord, thank you."

As I conclude this chapter, allow me to provide a little bit of context on my thoughts of the last sentence of my journal excerpt. What the gift of time brought me was answers and clarity. The man I thought was my husband (at that time) was not. The woman I am today would have never chose someone like him. I learn that your dreams and desires changes as you mature and get older. At that time, I had a different interpretation of what I thought those witnesses meant in regards to the statement that I would be glad that I waited. I thought they were referring to the one I thought would be my husband. But, what the gift of time brought me was a completely different perspective. I can see now that I would be glad that I waited on the one God has for me and not what I thought I wanted at that time. Praise God!

CHAPTER 5

Unexpected Blessings in Brokenness

"The Lord will perfect that which concerneth me..."

—Psalms 138:8 (KJV)

I want to paint a picture for you. After reading the following scenario, close your eyes and visualize the scenario. Choose an animal of your choice. You recognize that the animal has been abandoned, abused, or neglected in some way. You clearly recognize that the animal is hurting. The animal is limping. You can see visible bruises. Perhaps there may be internal bruises as well. Your heart immediately fills with compassion for the animal. You act to rescue or bring the animal to a place of safety. In some cases, you may desire to take the animal home or adopt. You want to provide food, shelter, love, safety, and security. You are walking towards the animal, getting close in physical proximity. Acting with only the animal's best interest in mind, you reach out to help or rescue the animal. However, instead of the animal receiving the help or rescue, the animal becomes afraid and begins to feel threatened. The animal feels insecure. What do you think happens next? Perhaps, the animal begins to growl, bark, run away, or launches toward you. You respond in one of two ways. You either take steps back to protect yourself or ignore the warnings given by the animal. If the latter is the case, you may end up getting bit or hurt in some way. Your intentions were to help and rescue, not bring further hurt to the animal. However, the animal does not see your best intentions. The animal only remembers its experiences of how it was treated by the people that hurt it. This is the animal's frame of reference and experiences with people. They remember the pain, the hurting, and the suffering. They associate the pain, hurting, and suffering with people. "People hurt me. Therefore, I experience pain and suffering." The animal thinks they are in danger of being hurt again. By instinct, the animal reacts or behaves in a way to protect or keep itself from being hurt. What do you think? As you read the scenario, did any of it sound familiar? Do you know anyone like this? I did. I recognized myself and many other people that I have encountered in my life.

No One Exempt

Pain and brokenness will come to all of us at one time or another in our lives. No one is exempt. Pain and brokenness will come to the righteous as well as the unrighteousness (Matthew 5:45). We live in a sin-cursed and fallen world, and eventually we will crash into one another. I do not believe that pain and brokenness were a part of God's original plan for us. Remember Adam and Eve in the Garden of Eden? I believed God wanted to protect us from the sin, curses, pain, and brokenness. I believe this is why God gave Adam and Eve specific instructions concerning the tree in the garden (I will discuss this in more detail later in this chapter). Since Adam and Eve did not obey these instructions, they had to suffer the consequences: the consequences of knowing sin, pain, cursedness, and brokenness. Centuries later, we are still suffering from Adam and Eve's disobedience as a result of what happened that day in the garden. In chapter 1, I shared some of my experiences with pain and brokenness in my past relationships. Obviously, going through these experiences were painful. However, in my experience, what was even more painful was waiting for the healing process to be complete. The healing process is slow, sometimes unbearable. Your flesh is irritated, and it cries with agony. Your flesh suffers. You walk around with the pain. You eat with the pain. You go to sleep with the pain and wake up with the pain. You cannot escape the pain because it is constantly reminding you of what happened that caused the pain in the first place. I know brokenness. We are close relatives. Brokenness is familiar to me, and I am familiar with it. Remember Jesus? Isaiah 53:3 states, "He was despised and rejected by men, a man of sorrows and familiar with suffering" (NIV). Jesus knows pain, brokenness, and suffering as well. I take comfort in knowing that Jesus can identify even more so with our pain, brokenness, and suffering. Maybe this is what Paul meant when he said in Philippians 3:10, "I want to know Christ and the power of his resurrection and the fellowship of sharing in his sufferings, becoming like him in his death" (NIV). When we experience our own pain, brokenness, and suffering, we share in the fellowship of suffering with Christ. As a result, we are more close to him. Psalm 34:18, 51:17, and Isaiah 57:15 talks about the Lord being close to those of a broken and contrite heart. Alternatively, Thank God, I know the other side of pain, brokenness, and suffering. I know what it is like for the healing process to reach completeness. No one, I don't think, likes to look at themselves and see broken pieces all over the place. It is painful to look at, embarrassing, and sometimes shameful. I have had many conversations with God regarding this very topic. On many occasions, I would pour out my heart to him and tell him that I am tired of feeling and being broken. I do not want to be broken no longer. It hurts too much. It is sad, and it does not feel good. Help me break free so I do not experience brokenness in this area of my life again.

Looks Familiar?

What does brokenness feel like to you? To me, brokenness feels like being in a dry place. You are moving forward, but barely. There are no signs of life in this dry place. You feel stuck. Some of my internal thoughts were "How do I rise up out of this place"? Brokenness feels like going around in the same circle over and over again. The landscape (although in dry places such as the desert, there is hardly landscape) begins to look familiar. The landmarks (bushes, rocks, boulders, etc.) also look familiar. You are beginning to come to your senses and say to yourself, "Wait a minute. I have been here before. I am tired of seeing the same things over and over again." If you are tired of it enough, you get to the place where you begin to ask the Lord to help you get out of the rut. You no longer want to experience the same old patterns anymore. You recognize these patterns are no longer good for you. You recognize the patterns are holding you back. Instead of the patterns building you up, they are tearing you down, repressing you, and keeping you from growing and maturing emotionally and/or spiritually. Does any of this resonate with you? I added this chapter to the book because I believe God does not want us to experience brokenness for the rest of our lives. I do not believe God wants us to experience feeling crappy and bad about ourselves for the rest of our lives.

Did not Jesus say that he came that we would have life and life more abundantly (John 10:10)? God does want us to walk in freedom and victory over brokenness. However, before we can obtain freedom and victory from the broken areas in our lives, we may have to experience more brokenness. I know this statement does not make sense, but I will explain what I mean in the subsequent section.

More Brokenness

Does God allow pain and brokenness? Deuteronomy 32:39 states, "I have wounded and I will heal" (NIV). Job 5:18, states, "For he wounds, but he also binds up; he injures, but his hands also heal" (NIV). There is purpose in pain and brokenness. I think of a skillful surgeon that cuts into our bodies and wounds in order to bring healing to the area of the body that needs it. It is the same way with God. He cuts, wounds, and removes in order to bring emotional and spiritual healing and growth. So yes, He allows the pain and brokenness. When God heals the cuts and wounds, we will heal in a way where we will never experience brokenness in that area of our life again. Here's another example. Think about a leg that has been broken. If the break was not a clean break, doctors have to rebreak the leg in order for the leg to heal properly. In terms of our brokenness, God allows the re-break so that we can heal properly. These analogies have been the story of my life. I feel like I have been either on crutches or laid on the surgical table and kept on it for a long time, decades. Soon after a storm would end came another one.

I felt like the pain and brokenness that I experienced brought me more pain and brokenness. How so? Since I had experienced hurt and brokenness, unaware, I would function from this place of brokenness. I would make dysfunctional decisions/choices from this place of brokenness. The way I experienced people and saw the world were through the lenses of pain and brokenness. I would attract people with their own pain and brokenness, and what do you know, somehow I would get caught up in their dysfunctional messes. As a result of my dysfunctional lenses (sight) and decisions, I would experience more pain and brokenness on top of the pain and brokenness that was already there. It seemed like God was saying, "Enough!" He worked a plan for me to be free and healed once and for all so that I would grow emotionally and spiritually and not have to keep repeating these dysfunctional patterns for the rest of my life. Like any loving parent, you allow your children to experience hurt so they can learn and grow from the experiences. God allowed the brokenness in order for me to heal completely. I guess I had to learn the hard way because I was not getting it or seeing the dysfunctional patterns. After you have experienced pain and brokenness time after time, you get to the place where you look up and say, "Okay, Lord, you got my attention." An internal dialogue begins and questions like "Why do I keep going through this?" "What am I doing wrong?" "What is wrong with me?" "Why do I allow people to treat me this way?" and so on. When one gets to this place, one is hopefully ready for change. One is hopefully ready to do whatever one needs to do so that one will not have to experience more pain and brokenness. Have you or do you know someone that has experienced this exact process? One thing began to be clear for me. There was a plan and purpose in my pain and brokenness. I sometimes wonder if God could have used other methods to perfect his work in me (Psalms 138:8). Pain does not feel good. However, God uses the pain to get our attention and perfect his work in us.

UNEXPECTED BLESSINGS IN BROKENNESS

Unexpected Blessings

The morning I began this chapter, I woke up to the lyrics of a song produced and recorded in the seventies by gospel singer Andrae Crouch. The chorus of the song states, "Through it all, through it all, I learn to trust in Jesus, I learn to trust in God." I suspect Mr. Crouch knew something about pain and brokenness. As I meditated on the words of this song, I knew the Lord was speaking to me about my brokenness. As I reflected on all the brokenness that I experienced, I can say that the very words of Mr. Crouch's song ring true for me. As a result of being broken time after time, I got to the place where I learned to trust in Jesus, and I learned to trust in God. I emphasize the word *learn* because I did not always understand why God would allow me to experience pain, hurt, and brokenness. This was a peculiar phenomenon to me. I mean, for Pete's sake, he is God. "Do something," I would say to Him. "Did you see that? Did you see how that person treated me? Did you see how that person hurt me? I am hurting here! Help me. Stop the pain and hurting." At that time, my internal dialogue stemmed from my new relationship with God. I thought that as long as I obeyed God, cross my t's, and dot my i's, I would be safe from experiencing pain and hurt. Other people would have pain and hurt, but not me. I was in for a rude awakening. Clearly, I needed a good dose of maturity. Clearly, I did not understand how kingdom principles work. As I matured in God, I began to develop a God perspective about pain and brokenness. I learned that brokenness is not all bad. Yes, it is painful to experience; however, there can be unexpected blessings in brokenness. I experienced these unexpected blessings. After the storms had passed, I would take the time to reflect on some of my most painful and broken seasons. I would say to myself, "Yeah, I can see why I needed to go through that." Would I want to experience the pain and hurt all over again? No; however, I can appreciate the refining and perfecting process as a result of the pain and brokenness. I believe God uses (Romans 8:28) the pain and brokenness to bring growth and maturity. Apparently, I needed a lot of that and then some.

Lessons Learned from Brokenness

One cannot experience pain and brokenness and not learn a single thing. One cannot experience pain and brokenness without learning their purpose in their life. The things I learned from my own pain and brokenness were invaluable lessons. I will jump right to the lessons I learned. Note the following ten lessons:

1. One cannot minister to the broken if you have not experienced brokenness yourself. God works all of our pain and brokenness together for our good (Romans 8:28).
2. Pain has a purpose, and whether we like pain or not, God uses pain to get our attention. He gets our attention in order to prefect us (Psalm 138:8).
3. I learned about God's way. If you think you have God figured out, think again. "For my thoughts are not your thoughts, neither are your ways my ways. As the heavens are higher than the earth, so are my ways higher than your ways and my thoughts than your thoughts" (Isaiah 55:8–9, NIV). God will not always do things the way you think he will do things. When he shows you something, he may not carry out the plan the way you think the plan will be carried out. I have been surprised many times by God with an unexpected outcome. Because of these experiences, I learned to wait on God, keep pace with him, and not get ahead of him.

4. I learned about God's character. He does not change or lie. People do. Hebrews 6:18 states, "God did this so that, by two unchangeable things in which it is impossible for God to lie, we who have fled to take hold of the hope offered to us may be greatly encouraged" (NIV). What are the two unchangeable things? The two unchangeable things are His word (promises) and he swore in blood (blood covenant). When God gives you a promise and he confirms it in his word, it is good as gold. "For ever, O Lord, thy word is settled [a done thing, for sure] in heaven" (Psalm 119:89, KJV). What I have learned is that even though God's word is settled in heaven, it is not always settled here on earth in our hearts.

5. I discovered a close and intimate relationship with the Lord. "I am my beloved and he is mine" (Song of Songs 6:3, NIV). "The Lord is close to the brokenhearted and saves those who are crushed in spirit" (Psalms 34:18, NIV). A broken heart, being crushed and, in some translations, contrite, were ingredients that brought me a close/intimate relationship with Lord God. Though I do not recommend that you go out and put yourself in harm's way or make unwise decisions. I do recommend that when the pain and brokenness comes (not if but when), you allow the process. You will reap wonderful by-products as a result of the pain and brokenness.

6. I learned that you love people the way God would love you. 1 Peter 4:8 states, "Most important of all, continue to show deep love for one another, for love covers a multitude of sins" (NIV). It is easy to love someone that loves you back or reciprocate. The test is to love someone that is difficult to love or makes it difficult to love. Jesus said in Matthew 5:44-48, "Love your enemies…if you love those who love you, what rewards will you get?" (NIV).

7. As a result of my own brokenness, I began to see people the way God sees them. When I am having difficulty forgiving, I ask God to show me how He sees the person. When

God shows me the other person's brokenness, it helps me to release that person. I no longer see the injury that the person inflicted upon me. I now see the person as broken and in need of their own healing. Psalms 36:9 states, "In your light we see light" (NIV). In addition, Psalm 119:130 states, "The entrance of they words giveth light; it giveth understanding unto the simple" (KJV). The next time you are having difficulty forgiving someone, ask God to show you how he sees that person. You will be amazed by God's revelation.

8. I learned that God's will does not always come to pass because people make choices (remember the story of Mr. Perfectionist, chapter 1). When God made us, he made us with a free will. He wanted us to have the freedom to choose. God reveals his perfect will for our lives, but it up to us to choose his perfect will. For example, 2 Peter 3:9 states that "the Lord is not slow in keeping his promise, as some understand slowness. He is patient with you, not wanting anyone to perish, but everyone to come to repentance" (NIV). God presents salvation to an individual. It is now up to the individual to open the door of his or her heart to choose salvation. Some people will choose, and some will not. God does not want anyone to perish (go to hell). He wants us all with him in eternity. It saddens and breaks God's heart to see people rejecting his will for them. But what can he do? He gave man the ability and freedom to choose (free will). I learned that sometimes brokenness occurs in our lives because of someone else's choice in rejecting God's will for their life. As a result, the person who knows the will of God suffers because of someone else's inability to hear accurately, disobedience, or poor choices.

9. I learned that God does not always reveal every detail about his will. We do not always know what God knows. We are only responsible for what God said to us. Remember Adam and Eve? God specifically told Adam and Eve which

tree to eat from and which tree to avoid. You know the story. Eve was deceived by the serpent. Adam and Eve ate from the forbidden tree. Genesis 3:4 states, "'You will not die,' the serpent said to the woman. 'For God knows that when you eat of it your eyes will be opened and you will be like God, knowing good and evil'" (NIV). Obviously, this was lie. God did not want Adam and Eve eating from the tree of knowledge of good and evil because he stated in Genesis 2:17, "For when you eat of it you will surely die [instant spiritual separation from God and subsequent physical death]" (NIV). God had a reason for Adam and Eve to not eat from the tree of knowledge of good and evil. If only Adam and Eve had just done what God said. Brokenness comes into our life when we attempt to do what God knows instead of what God said. We are responsible for what God said and not what He knows. We will never entirely know what God knows. Paul said in 1 Corinthians 13:12, "For now, we see through a glass, darkly; but then face to face: now I know in part; but then shall I know even as also I am known" (KJV). Word to the wise, do what God said, nothing more and nothing less. You may experience no more brokenness than necessary.

10. Finally, one evening God revealed an issue in an area of my life that I was unaware of. I will share a journal excerpt dated January 3, 2013. I will then follow up in subsequent paragraphs by sharing some of my reflections (meditations) and thoughts I believe the Lord was revealing to me on that day.

> "I pull away from people and isolate myself when I experience changes and abandonment in the friendship. I do this when I have been especially close to the person. I pull away from people I do not trust. I do not give them another chance to hurt me."

FINDING LOVE IN ALL THE RIGHT PLACES

As I meditated on these words, my heart began to speak to me: this is accurate. My mind reflected back on a few close relationships that are no more. Now, I understand why it was hard for me to accept changes. I can be rigid, a slight need for control. I like predictability. I admit I am a creature of habit. I am forty-two years old, and I am just coming to this awakening. It is clear. This is an issue of stability and security. Apparently, these components were not solidified (foundation) as a child. This is one developmental stage I did not master (trust versus mistrust, attachment issues). When parents are broken, they create broken babies, babies who become children, children who become adolescents, and adolescents who become adults. Whatever developmental milestones you do not master as a child, you somehow attempt (conscious or unconscious) to compensate for it in other people or things.

Unaware, I sought stability and security in my close relationships. I grew up experiencing changes and instability. We moved a lot. We struggled financially. Sometimes we had food to eat, and sometimes we did not. My family and I lacked many things growing up. I do not know what it was like to have new clothes for school. I earned the second highest score on the junior high drill team tryouts. That day, I had a little dose of self-esteem and confidence. But since my parents could not afford to pay for my uniforms or send me to drill camp, I had to drop out. I could not be on the team. My biological father abandoned and rejected me before I was born. My stepfather, who raised me since I was one year old, mistreated me. Due to my early experiences, I think this why I do not like it when close relationships change or people change. I realize it's not their fault. They have their own path to pursue. Life goes on. Heal me, Lord. I do not want to be like this. I cannot expect people to cater to me, build their life around me. They have their own life to live and their own God paths to follow. They are not responsible for my needs. I do not get my stability and security from them. In reflection, I understand why I would get irritated, angry, and sad at those who were close to me. They had left or the friendship changed at some point. I opened my heart to them, trusted them with it, and they walked away. They walked away to pursue their own life. The lesson I am learning is that stability and security come from God, not man. Lord, heal me and make me whole. I do not want to be like this.

A friend sent me the lyrics of a song on December 31, 2012. I believe this song was godsent, perfect timing. The song was written by Misty Edwards and is called "I Knew What I was Getting Into / All Men Are Broken." Misty prophetically sings the lyrics as if God was singing it or saying it himself. The lyrics state, "All men are broken and broken men break their children who grow up to be broken." Wow! The song goes on to say, "I am bigger than that." I take comfort in these words. God is bigger than that. Yes, God is bigger than that. No matter how much brokenness I have experienced, God is bigger. He is bigger than any amount of brokenness that I have experienced. He is more than able to heal and restore. His power is sufficient (2 Corinthians 12:9), ashes for beauty (Isaiah 61:3).

As I conclude this chapter, I want you to think about your own brokenness. I shared some of my experiences and what I learned so far in this journey we call life. God specializes in taking broken pieces and creating a beautiful mosaic masterpiece. I leave you with two questions. Do you know your life's lessons regarding your own brokenness? What do you think God wants you to learn from your pain and brokenness? I exhort you. If you want the right kind of love to find you, facing, getting healed from, and getting free from your brokenness are imperative.

CHAPTER 6

> "As water reflects a face, so a man's
> heart reflects the man."
>
> —Proverbs 27:19 (NIV)

One morning, I woke up to a popular song sung by the late Whitney Houston. I heard the words, "The greatest love of all, it's easy to achieve, learning to love yourself is the greatest love of all." For several more days, I would wake up to the same song, hearing the same lyrics. I began to wonder what was the meaning or what was God trying to say to me. I did not understand the full significance then, but now it is clear. The lesson I realized and learned was that I needed to love myself more. And what this meant was that I needed to not make room (physically) or allow in my space (emotionally and spiritually) toxic or any type of dysfunctional relationship that would impede growth, disrupt, tear down, or destroy my life. I needed to learn to set in place appropriate boundaries on things and/or people that were not healthy for me. I needed to be mindful of who and what I was investing my time in.

FINDING LOVE IN YOURSELF

    I talked about in chapter 1 that finding love in the right place begins with first finding love in Jesus. This chapter essentially echoes the same message. Once you have found love in Jesus, it is time to work on finding love in yourself. If you are healthy emotionally and spiritually, then you will attract people who are healthy emotionally and spiritually. The same principle applies in waiting on God for the right spouse. It is important to not only have the ability to receive love, but you must be able to give it as well. We need to be healthy enough to receive love and healthy enough to give love. In essence, you cannot give what you do not possess, and what you do not possess, you are not healthy enough to receive. As I reflect back over the past years of my life, God had been perfecting this very process in me. Unbeknownst to me, God was teaching me to love, respect, cherish, and value myself. God used the heartbreaks that I experienced in my former relationships with men to teach me these virtues. Today, I am glad that he saw the whole picture and worked his plan for my life (Jeremiah 33:3). I remember being so focused on just getting through or rather around the heartbreak that I was not aware of the work God was doing internally. I also needed emotional healing from wounds experienced as a child. God saw that I needed to be healed and whole from the negative experiences in which I grew up in. While I won't take the time to share the things that I had experienced, these negative experiences impacted and shaped my life psychologically, emotionally, socially, relationally, and spiritually. I believe that we can become products of our environment. I was a product of the things I had experienced. One time (in an attempt to help my brother through his own pain) my brother said to me, "Be patient with me. I am this way because the world [family, friends, etc.] made me this way." Those hurtful experiences impacted him socially, financially, emotionally, spiritually, and even physically. I remember those words my brother said to me that day. God is patient with us as we wrestle through our issues. He knows and understands the root causes, and he has a plan for freedom!

My painful experiences left me broken to the point that I did not know who I was or who I was in Christ. I was highly insecure, had low self-esteem, low self-worth, and a very low self-image. I did not know I was made in God's image, and I did not know God's purpose and plan for my life. I did not know I was fearfully and wonderfully made (Psalm 139:14). I remember always feeling bad about myself. I felt miserable and felt trapped in the misery. Because of these issues, I would attract dysfunctional and unhealthy relationships, which left me more broken. When an individual has suffered a wrong or has been affected by hurtful experiences, the individual operates from this place of hurt, whether he/she is aware of it or not. We make choices and behave from this place of hurt. Man quickly judges these choices and behaviors, but God knows the source(s) from which decisions and behaviors originate. In other words, he understands the motivations behind our decisions and behaviors. He sees, and his heart is filled with love and compassion. He pursues us relentlessly to get us to see ourselves the way he sees us. If we allow him, he desires to bring healing and wholeness. The key word is *if*, which means that our healing and wholeness are conditional. It is based upon our free will to choose and surrender to God's plan for restoration. Sometimes God's plan of restoration involves pain, and pain does not feel good. It means that we have to willingly place ourselves on the surgical table (without anesthesia) and allow God to remove the things that he knows will hinder and stunt our growth emotionally and spiritually. We cannot fool or hide from God. He sees it, and he targets the area. This means we may have to face some things that we have ran from, repressed, swept under the rug, or avoided altogether. In reality, these are defense mechanisms, and as a professor of psychology and counseling, I understand that the purpose of defense mechanisms is to protect and preserve. From a psychological point of view, I get it. Because someone did not do a good job of protecting and preserving, we set up defense mechanisms to keep from being hurt or feeling the hurt. However, from a spiritual point of view, God is more than capable of protecting and preserving. Therefore, we do not need defense mechanisms. If he is asking for a certain area of your life, give it to him. You may experience the pain of having to go through or relive the experience(s), but God is right there with you while you face the giants in your life. There is no other way to be healed and whole. You cannot go around the pain; you must go through pain. Dr. Sandra Wilson explained it best, "Hurt people hurt people." When you have unresolved emotional issues, you will inevitably hurt someone else, and sometimes in the same way you were hurt, whether intentional or unintentional. To further keep from hurting yourself and others, get healing and become healthy.

God is not trying to withhold his blessings from our lives (Psalms 84:11). He wants us to have the blessings as much as we desire the blessings; however, God will not give us something or someone which we are not ready or prepared to receive. I remember watching Bishop T. D. Jakes on the Television Broadcast Network (TBN). He gave a perfect example. He said he would not give the keys to the car and trust a five-year-old to go to the store in the same way he would trust an adult. The obvious difference is that the five-year-old is not ready or capable of driving, let alone going to the store by himself. The car is mechanically able; however, the five-year-old is not. A blessing given too soon or too early can become not a blessing. Instead, the blessing can hurt you. The blessing that was meant to bless you can now be not good for you. This analogy is the same with God. God wants to heal and make us whole before he brings the blessing. When God blesses, he adds no sorrow to it (Proverbs 10:22). This may mean that you may have to wait longer than you planned or expected in order to be ready for the blessing. I often see and hear too many stories about people in relationships who are dating, engaged, or married wrestling with unresolved broken issues. It is the usual outcome. The relationship suffers and, in some cases, dissolves. Case in point, I went to visit my mother and stepfather during Christmas 2012. I stayed up late one night to watch one of my favorite television shows that my mother had been recording for me. My mother had already gone to bed. Later on, she came out of her room, and I asked her what she was doing up. She saw that somebody was up but really came out to turn on the house alarm. After she did her duties, she proceeded to sit on the sofa, and we started to talk as we always do. She wanted me to pray and began to tell me about an individual that was experiencing difficulties in their marriage. After some time in conversation and prayer with my mom, she later went to bed. As I pondered on our conversation, I thanked God that I was not married. I'd rather remain single or marry at a later age than marry with issues of brokenness. I'd rather wait on the Lord to bring healing and wholeness before I marry. The lesson that I learned in this conversation was that it does not pay to marry someone that is broken or marry if you are broken. In the long run and, in some marriages, the short run, the brokenness will eventually affect the marriage. Marriage or getting married is no cure to fixing someone that is broken or fixing your own brokenness. How many times have you heard people say "I thought that if we married, it would have solved our problems" or "If we got married, things would have gotten better or he/she would change"? Frankly, this is not realistic thinking, and as I said in the introduction, there is nothing new under the sun. It is the same script, just different characters. I have seen through friends and family what can happen when we take the shortcut, the easy way, or compromise. The end result is never favorable. As far as this individual's marriage, I believe God has a plan to bring healing, wholeness, and restoration. I do wonder, however, what the marriage would be like had they both waited to marry and worked on self-issues, allowing God to bring healing and wholeness. Would they have suffered as much in their marriage? I exhort you to work on you before love finds you. Allow time for personal development and growth. The time to heal and be whole may take longer depending on how much brokenness you have experienced. Nevertheless, God is willing to heal and bring wholeness, providing that you submit to the process. This means investing the time to work on your issues.

I learned something else. People make the best choice they can with what they know at the time. They make choices and function from that place of darkened understanding. I like to use the analogy from the movie *Crash*. We walk around crashing into one another trying to fulfill or meet a need/desire to belong, be loved, and be accepted. These needs are normal. God made us with the desire to connect with one another. He made us for relationships. However, the problem with crashing into one another in order to meet those needs outside of God is that we sometimes end up hurting ourselves more and the other person in an attempt to meet that need. Now, the wounds are even deeper. This is not God's plan that we crash into one another in order to get those needs met. God is more than capable of fulfilling those needs, but we must allow him to fulfill the needs according to his plan and his way. He wants us to be healthy and whole. When we meet the person we were intended to meet, we do not have to crash or hurt them. We can enjoy the relationship and enjoy the blessing.

CHAPTER 7

Investing in a Healthier You

> "Beloved, I wish above all things
> that thou mayest prosper and be in health,
> even as thy soul prospereth."
>
> —3 John: 1 (KIV)

I mentioned in the previous chapter that it is important to allow time for personal development and growth and to allow time for healing and wholeness. If you allow this process, you will eventually learn to love yourself. And the best way to begin loving yourself, is to begin investing in you. You may be wondering, what does that look like? Well, this chapter is essentially about investing in a healthier you. I will not provide you with a step-by-step process or some formula. I will, however, discuss some general guidelines that can apply to anyone. The reason I will not provide a step-by-step process or formula because personal development and growth will vary from individual to individual. It will look differently because each individual's situation is unique. There may be some commonalities and/or parallels, but each situation is unique to the individual.

In the following sections, In the following sections, I will discuss some general guidelines that helped me obtained freedom, healing and wholeness in deficit areas of my life.

Take Inventory

The first suggestion that I recommend is to take inventory of your life. Write a list of the issues that you know if you did not resolve. These issues could affect you and how you function in relationships for the rest of your life. Think about matters of the heart or unresolved issues that you have been avoiding or neglecting. Have you noticed patterns or habits in which you find yourself in yet another dysfunctional and/or unhealthy relationship? Start with these issues. Remember the saying "You attract outwardly who you are internally"? If you want the right kind of love to find you, you have to be that person. Healthy love cannot find you if there are unresolved, unhealthy issues within you. If you are a mess, you will attract unhealthy relationships, and unhealthy relationships mean unhealthy love. One area in which I needed to take inventory had to do with relationships with men. I remember asking myself (after yet another failed relationship), Why do I keep attracting the same type of man? What is it about me that attract these types of men? I was so tired of the same type of man finding me. I told the Lord I cannot continue to keep getting my heart broken. What am I doing wrong? I needed answers and insight so that I would not find myself in the same type of relationship. I was ready for a change because getting my heart broken was becoming old. Naively, in my early twenties, I thought that dating a man who was a Christian would mean that I would be safe. I learned the hard way that just because someone is a Christian does not mean they are safe to date. One evening I sat up late to ponder on the answers to the aforementioned questions. The one thing that I came to realize was that these men were like my biological father, who abandoned and rejected me before I was born, and stepfather, who raised me since I was one year old. I realized these men had the following issues in common:

1. Emotionally and/or spiritually immature
2. Unresolved issues or unhealthy boundaries with ex-girlfriends (I would always find myself in these love triangles.)
3. Unresolved issues with their fathers
4. Did not have financial stability or job/career stability (constantly changing jobs)
5. Confused and fickle (His words were incongruent with his behavior and/or follow-through.)
6. Some type of abuse, abandonment, and/or rejection issues
7. Struggled with identity issues
8. Lacked discernment in his own life
9. Insecure, low self-esteem, low self-confidence, and low self-worth
10. Relationship did not last longer than three to six months

Taking inventory will require introspection and time with the Lord. Some of these patterns and habits are deep-seated and/or rooted while others are not as deep-seated and/or rooted. I hope my example of taking inventory has been helpful to you. Now, it is your turn.

Face the Brokenness

One thing I learned about pain and suffering was how we respond to the process. Pain can deform or cause you to conform. Your response to pain will determine which it will be. This type of pain and suffering can make or cause people to turn away from God, get angry at God, develop other coping mechanisms outside of God, and cause suicidal tendencies. Pain can separate you from

God, causing you to distance or isolate yourself, or the pain can cause you to run towards him, hold on to him, and cleave to him. When we respond in the latter, it is in these moments intimacy is developed. It is important how we respond to pain. God won't put more on us than we are able to bear, even though it feels like we cannot bear it. God filters these circumstances through his loving hands. He said he will be with us through the valley of the shadow of death. If God is calling you to a season of pain and suffering, you are in his will. His presence is where you want to be. If he is in the desert or wilderness, then there you shall be. If he is in the rain, then there you shall be. We all have our own crosses to carry. We will have to die to our flesh and surrender our will. Pain and suffering produce a harvest of righteousness. Just remember pain and suffering have a purpose. Father God knows how you feel. Knowing how other people felt or feel makes the difference. Remember pain and suffering is understood by not only Job and Jesus but others, such as the apostles, in the Bible as well. Jesus knows the wounds of relational pain. He knows how you feel. Everyone can identify with pain. Pain is a universal language that we can share and experience. Race and cultures are not all exempt from this process. God does not want us to become stuck in the pain or suffering, but he does want us to mature, become strengthened, and gain a perspective on the process of pain and suffering. Another song comes to mind as I write this passage: "This is my story, this is my song, praising my savior all the day long. This is my story. This is my song. Praising my savior all the day long. Perfect submission all is at rest." Sometimes, your flesh does not want to go through the pain and suffering, but this is where surrendering your will comes into play.

Once you have identified the issue(s) and have obtained insight from the Lord, it is time to work through the issue(s). I once heard someone say while watching a television interview, the interviewee said, "Find the fear in the room and face it." That statement struck me because there is much validity to the statement. It is with this premise that I say to you. Whatever the issue may be, find it and face it. Pray for God's strength and God's courage. It can be difficult or painful to face yourself or the issues. The tendency may be to run due to fear, shame, or embarrassment. Don't you dare run away! If you do, you will just be delaying the inevitable. When I did not think I would make it to the day I would finish my PhD, God admonished me with Philippians 4:13. I admonish you with the same passage. You can do all things through Christ who gives you the strength. Remember earlier in the chapter in which I told you that I wrestled with insecurity and low self-esteem? Being insecure and having low self-esteem is like walking around carrying bad news all the time. Internally, I literally felt sad, bad, and inferior. Feeling this way did not feel good at all. It was like a weight that weighed on me so heavily (Hebrews 12:1). I got to the place where I was ready to be free from the feeling. I no longer wanted to carry the weight around. I had wrestling moments with God where he would show me the way he saw me. I had days in which God and I did not see eye to eye. It took me some time to see myself the way God saw me; nevertheless, God's power and relentless pursuit of me prevailed. If he is for you, who can be against you (Romans 8:31)? If you got the faith, he got the power. Today, I am free from those insecurities, low self-esteem, and low self-confidence.

Confess

James 5:16 states, "Confess your faults to one another, and pray for one another, that ye may be healed. The effectual fervent prayer of a righteous man availeth much" (KJV). Once you have taken inventory and are ready to face the issue, the next step is to confess. Confess openly the issue(s) to God. Even though He is already aware of the issue(s), the purpose of confession, according to James (through the inspiration of the Holy Spirit), is to bring healing. You are also involving God in the process of your healing and restoration. You need his help. You cannot be healed and restored without him. Confession is also about acknowledging the issue and that you no longer will hide or run from the issue. In addition, confession takes away the power of the enemy in using the issue over you. Once the issue has been exposed, freedom awaits you. He who the Son sets free is free indeed (John 8:36). This is what the enemy does not want us to do. He does not want us to confess because he knows that once the issue(s) has been exposed, we become free. The enemy does not want us to be free. He wants us to continue walking in chains and in bondages. I say choose freedom. In addition to confessing to God, share/confess with someone in whom you trust and can hold you accountable while praying for you. Be honest and transparent. Confession is powerful and cleansing to the soul. It is like sweeping, gathering up the trash, and dumping the trash in a garbage bin, only for it to be picked up and carried away on trash day. You will never see the trash again. Like God, when we confess, we dump the issue, and God carries it away (Psalm 103:12). No matter how painful or embarrassing the issue, trust God through the healing process. Remember, in order to heal and be whole, you will need to go through the valley and not around it. God is with you. My prayer for you is 3 John 3:2, "Beloved, I wish above all thing that thou mayest prosper and be in health, even as your soul (mind, will, emotions) prospereth" (KJV).

Release

Once you confess the issue, the next step is to let go of the issue(s), which means you need to work on moving forward and not looking back. You will have to work on not picking up or carrying the issue again. It has already been given to God; however, there may be triggers, such as a place, a scent, a phrase, a song, or a person's name, that may cause the issues(s) to resurface. If this is the case, know your triggers and work on releasing the individual(s) that hurt you. Whenever someone has been hurt or injured, usually issues of unforgiveness or lack of self-forgiveness may be present. Assess where you fall on this spectrum. Forgiveness does not mean you forget or are condoning what the individual(s) did to you. It means you are making a conscious choice (exercising your free will) to release the individual and the hurt. The individual owes you nothing, and in time your emotions will catch up to your conscious decision to forgive. You may have to release the individual and the hurt on a moment-to-moment, day-to-day, or week-to-week basis; nevertheless, you can do it. I once heard a speaker (Linda Lange, Life Applications Ministries, www.lifeapplicationsministries.org) say that when you do not forgive, you continue to pass on the legacy of the person that hurt you. In essence, what you do not forgive, you give. When we do not forgive and release, the individual(s) continues to have power in your life. I recommend that you ask God to help you forgive. Utilize your support system to help you in the process of releasing and forgiving. One night, I was experiencing some sadness. There was some unexpected news that triggered the sadness and reminded me of the individual that hurt me. A close/covenant friend who did not know what I was experiencing in the moment texted me Isaiah 61:3. The passage states, "To bestow on them a crown of beauty instead of ashes, the oil of gladness instead of mourning, and a garment of praise instead of a spirit of despair" (NIV). I pray and encourage you with the same passage. Lastly, I recommend that you research and find resource(s) that will help you understand what forgiveness means and what it looks like. It is important to forgive because when we do not forgive, neither will our heavenly father forgives us (Mark 11:26, NJV).

Walk with God

How can two walk together except when they agree (Amos 3:3)? God was and continues to be the glue that holds me together. As I reflect back on the pain and disappointments, it was God that kept me (from snapping, retaliating, etc.). I remember lying on the bathroom floor in my mother's home. The lights were off because I did not want anyone to know I was in there or hear me. It had been months since I broke up with my boyfriend at that time. I was in so much pain, and all I wanted to do was cry. I found a private place to do so, the bathroom. The pain was so intense that I had thoughts of wanting to die so that I could just stop hurting. In that moment, God met me. Even though God is spirit and not flesh and blood, it seemed as if he got down on his knees, knelt on the floor beside me, held me, and cried with me. At that moment, I was beginning to learn how to walk with God, discerning his voice and character. Nevertheless, I could feel the tangible presence of God in that bathroom on that day. I always refer back to that day in the bathroom because that was the day my life was changed. I discovered a relationship with God, and I experienced him in a real and tangible way. The pain did not go away overnight; however, in time, God picked me up off the bathroom floor that day to standing strong and tall. He brought me from that place of brokenness to healing. I wish I could tell you that after that defining moment, I did not experience more heartbreaks and disappointments, I did.

The difference was that I knew God was right there with me. From that defining moment, I knew I could walk with God. I knew he would take care of me. Whenever I found myself in trouble, pain, and more disappointments, I sought comfort in him immediately. God is the only one that knows exactly what to say and what to do. He knows how to bring perspective and make you feel better. God is never limited in his understanding and wisdom. He is all-knowing (omniscient), all-powerful (omnipotent), and everywhere at once (omnipresent). Friends and family mean well. They want the best for you, but sometimes they give bad or ungodly advice. They speak from their own negative experiences, and sometimes this is good (if they have been healed) and sometimes not so good (if healing has not occurred). I have also found that the very individuals that we esteem highly (pastors, teachers, prophets, etc.) are limited in their understanding and wisdom as well. Even though God has anointed them to serve in their appointed office, they are still not all-knowing, all-powerful, and everywhere at once. They are not God. I have seen pastors marry people that should have never been married. In fairness, what I also learned is that the individuals that we esteem highly cannot always discern the will of God for everyone; we are responsible for cultivating our own relationship with God and knowing God's will for our lives. As I write this passage, I hear these words in my spirit. It is an old hymn sang by Andrae Crouch: "Can't nobody do me Like Jesus, can't nobody do me like the Lord, can't nobody do me like Jesus, he's my friend."

    I exhort you to build a close, intimate relationship with God. Walk with him. Get to know him and develop a friendship. He is good at navigating troubled waters. You will never be disappointed. I can tell you that I have been walking with the Lord for over twenty-one years now. He has never disappointed me. I may not always understand his ways, and I may have times of wrestling with him, but in the end, he has never disappointed me. He is faithful, and faithful is he who promised (Hebrews 10:23, 1 Thessalonians 5:24, and 2 Thessalonians 3:3).

Prayer

Cover yourself in prayer. Once God reveals an area(s) of your heart that needs healing and restoring, spend time praying about these areas. Prayer is not easy. It is hard work. Prayer takes time and focused commitment. Let me warn you that sometimes your body may not naturally be inclined to always want to pray. Follow the spirit. Once you follow the spirit, the soul (will, mind, emotions) and body will come into an alignment. I can tell you that once you begin, you will be glad that you did, and after time, you will begin to see fruits as a result of a strong prayer life. In addition, healing does not necessarily come automatically. You have to initiate the healing process. A pastor I once knew said, knowing the will of God is not automatic. It is like driving a stick-shift automobile. In order for the automobile to move forward, you have to manually shift the gears. The gears will not shift on their own. I am using the same analogy concerning your healing. If you want healing, you will have to initiate healing. One way to initiate healing is through prayer. Prayer + faith + the power of God = results. Matthew 7:7–8 states, "Ask and it will be given to you; seek and you will find; knock and the door will be opened to you. For everyone who asks receives; he who seeks finds; and to him who knocks, the door will be opened" (NIV). I can tell you that I spent a lot of time bathing and soaking in prayer. I do not believe that I would be the person I am today if I had not spent time in prayer. By the way, a wonderful by-product of spending time in prayer is that you begin to establish an intimacy and closeness with God, a secret place. It is a place in your heart that no one (friends, family, etc.) can occupy, not even your future spouse. I will discuss more about what this means and what it looks like in the subsequent chapter.

God's Word Brings Healing

The healing and restoration process will require you to bathe in the word of God. God's word will penetrate the deep issues of your life that need healing. If it is a soul issue, God's word can bring healing. If it is a spiritual issue, God's word can bring healing. If it is a body (physical) issue, God's word can bring healing. Hebrews 4:12 states, "For the word of God is quick, and powerful and sharper than any two-edged sword, piercing even to the dividing asunder of soul [mind, will, emotions] and spirit, and of the joints and marrow [body], and is a discerner of the thoughts and intents of the heart" (KJV). In April 2005, I began to attend a church in Orange County, California. It was the same pastor that I mentioned earlier that referenced the will of God as a stick-shift automobile. He was the senior pastor and founder of the church. I loved everything about the church, the teachings, the worship, and the people. They were so friendly. I did not get involved in ministry right away. I sat for a year. I believed that God was giving me rest, and I gladly took the time off from serving in ministry as I had been very active at my former church. After the year was over, I began to get involved in ministries in which I felt the Lord was leading me to serve. In addition, the church had ongoing discipleship classes. Each class was named after a branch of the military. Each class was intense but, in retrospect, worth the effort. I would see individuals jumping in and taking the classes and becoming excited about what they were learning. Initially, I was not excited about the classes. People would invite me to take a class, but I was resistant. I saw the discipleship classes as another type of membership classes. I was thinking I was not going to go through another set of membership classes, and besides, I was fine. I did not need any more discipleship classes. I had already been through discipleship at my former church. Well, one day God began to speak to my heart, and he asked me to take the first level. Of course, I could not say no to God. I signed up for the next class. On the first day of class while the pastor was praying, tears began to stream down my face. I knew then God had something for me in the class. I am telling you, after the class had ended, my perception changed, and chains (mental and emotional bondages) broke off. I was free in certain areas of my life. I also grew in my relationship with the Lord, and I was discerning his voice, his character, and his ways. I got so hooked that I continued the discipleship program until I graduated. At the time I completed the program, there were five levels, and each level brought so much freedom and healing in places I was not aware. The mission of the church was simple, building solid lives. The discipleship classes were one method in becoming solid in the Lord. You see, when I first came to the church, I thought I was just fine and did not need any more discipleship; however, when I surrendered to the voice of God, I saw that I needed a lot more discipling. Healing and freedom were wonderful by-products of this discipleship program. I am not the same woman. I talk differently, see differently, and hear differently. I know who I am and who I am in the Lord. I know my spiritual gifts, my purpose, and my calling. God's word brings truth, wisdom, freedom, and revelation, just to name a few (Ephesians 1:17–18). I exhort you to trust God's word for your healing. "Now unto him that is able to do exceeding abundantly above all that we may ask or think according to the power that worketh in us" (Ephesians 3:20, KJV).

Finding Support

I could not have finished the journey God wanted for me without accountability from some trustworthy friends. The key word I emphasize is *trustworthy*. There will be individuals who will be in your outer circle, some in your inner circle, and then there is an inner-inner circle. I like to call the inner-inner circle as a typology of "behind the veil." You cannot trust everyone with sensitive, delicate matters of the heart. One of the requirements of the discipleship program that I mentioned in the previous section was for each participant to seek a covenant partner/friend. One role that the covenant friend played was to provide accountability in areas in which we revealed inner struggles. Covenant partners/friendship works, providing you are honest, transparent, and willing to be accountable. God sent me more than one accountability friend. They all had different purposes and served different roles in my life. Depending on whatever season of life I was weathering, each covenant friend had an important and purposeful role in my failures, wrestling moments with the Lord, healings, and victories. Aside from God, I could not have navigated these seasons without them. God used these friends to speak wisdom, revelation, healing, encouragement, truth, confession, intercession. I believe friendships that are heaven-sent are a gift from God and should be cherished. If you already have covenant-type friendships, I encourage you to invite them in your journey towards healing and wholeness. If you do not have covenant-type friendships, ask God to send you friends that are solid, mature, trustworthy, and in who you can be accountable. Ecclesiastes 4:9–10 (NIV) states, "Two are better than one, because they have a good return for their work: If one falls down, his friend can help him up. But pity the man who falls and has no one to help him!"

Seek Christian Resources

Hosea 4:6 states, "My people are destroyed for lack of knowledge" (KJV). I have a library full of books that I have read. Some of the books God led me to read and others I sought because I was desperate to understand the reason(s) why I was facing a particular issue. I can tell you that God used each book to bring revelation, insight, and understanding. Proverbs 2:1–6 states, "My son if you accept my words and store up my commands within you, turning your ear to wisdom and applying your heart to understanding, and if you call out for insight and cry aloud for understanding and if you look for it as for silver and search for it as for hidden treasure; then you will understand the fear of the Lord and find knowledge of God. For the Lord gives wisdom, and from his mouth come knowledge and understanding" (NIV). God used many Christian resources to bring insight and understanding about my issues. I believe that because I sought to arm myself with knowledge, I was no longer defeated. I encourage you to educate yourself about whatever issue, which Paul states can so easily beset you (Hebrews 12:1, KJV, NIV). I took a four-month deliverance and healing class (more than once) called Redeeming the Times (RTT) at my former church. The pastor and wife that oversaw this ministry were awesome people of God. They had walked through their own healing and restoration and now were helping others do the same. RTT's foundational textbook (along with a workbook) was called *Biblical Foundations of Freedom* by Art Mathais. This book helped me gain much healing, insight, understanding, and freedom. If you have the time, I recommend reading this book.

Biblical Counseling, Therapy, or Life Coaching

Sometimes, deep emotional wounds require specialized help. I am referring to counseling and/or therapy. There is a myth that counseling and/or therapy is for crazy people. This statement is not true and completely false. While working on my master's in clinical psychology at Azusa Pacific University, the program required each student to complete one year of individual therapy and one year of group therapy. I am glad that the university implemented this requirement in the program. It helped me to recognize my blind spots and that I am no more wounded than the person next door! Therefore, I can tell you that as a result of my therapeutic experiences, I was a much healthier person. It is okay to seek treatment. It does not mean you are crazy. Sometimes when issues are intense and overwhelming, we need someone that can be objective that can help us cope and find resolutions to our issues. Counseling and/or therapy can be beneficial in helping to alleviate symptoms while understanding the motivations behind why we do the things we do. If you find that you need specialized help with an issue(s), consult with a biblical/Christian counselor/therapist. Do your homework. Not all Christians who are licensed counselors/therapists/psychologists practice biblical/Christian counseling/therapy. You need someone who is Spirit-led, discerned, mature/wise in the word of God (can rightly divide the word of truth, 2 Timothy 2:15), and allows the ministry of the Holy Spirit to reveal, bring insight, and move freely.

An alternative to seeking help is life coaching. Again, not all Christians who are certified life coaches practice and/or implement biblical/Christian coaching methods. Essentially, the difference between a counselor/therapist/psychologist is that he or she works with the client to explore maladaptive patterns and dysfunctions that influence habits and behaviors. Sometimes exploring the past may be necessary, but not always. Counseling and/or therapy may require more time depending on how deep the wounds may be. Moreover, seeking life coaching services may not require a lot of time and does not necessarily involve explorations of the past. The focus is on the present and goal setting. Life coaches collaborate with individuals by helping them create goals for the present. Determine which approach best suits your needs. I recommend that you go the American Association of Christian Counselors website (www.aacc.net). On this website, you can find a Christian counselor/therapist and life coach where you live.

Allow Time

Lastly, as you consider the guidelines discussed above in your journey towards healing, remember that time heals all things. As you commit to your healing and a healthier you, you will need time. There is no way around this fact. For some of us, depending on how deep the wounds, it may take a little more time compared to others whose wounds may be superficial or less intense. Remember, time is your ally. Time is on your side. Just as the issues that you encountered did not spring up overnight, neither will your healing. It will be a journey. It will be a process. I have overcome a busload of issues that began when I was a baby in a crib. When I got of age and began to be accountable for my own life, I got to the place where I sought healing because I was tired of feeling the way I felt about myself and was tired of carrying the weight of dysfunction. Today, I am forty-five years old. God has done an amazing, supernatural work in my life. He has performed his work through a combination of the guidelines I have mentioned above. Remember when I mentioned that I took a four-month deliverance and healing class called Redeeming the Times (RTT)? One of the things that stuck with me in the class was that the healing process is like an onion layer. Once you think you have worked through an area and gained freedom, out of nowhere, another area comes to the surface. Do not be alarmed if this is the case. Deep emotional wounds sometimes have layers, and the deeper you go, the more healing you may discover. Exercise the fruits of the Spirit and be patient with the healing process and with yourself. Ecclesiastes 3:11 states, "He has made everything beautiful in his time" (NIV).

CHAPTER 8

While You Wait, Trust God for His Timing

"Then the Lord replied: 'Write down the revelation and make it plain on tablets so that a herald may run with it. For the revelation awaits an appointed time; it speaks of the end and will not prove false. Though it linger, wait for it; it will certainly come and will not delay.'"

—Habakkuk 2:2–3 (NIV)

The pain of releasing a dream and trusting God for a new one may be difficult (Isaiah 43:18–20). I learned that when we hold on so tightly to someone or something (whether we realize it or not), in a sense we are saying, "God, I don't trust you." It may sound harsh, but we need to be brutally transparent about the motives of our heart. Ladies, have you ever had to let go of a man you thought would be your husband? Men, have you ever had to let go of a woman you thought would be your wife? It is a difficult thing to do. There is a wrestling that takes place. Your emotions are screaming, "No, I want, I want..." And your heart is aching and breaking into pieces. Despite the emotional and physiological responses, God asks, and we must respond and surrender. If you have found yourself in this place, be encouraged; you are in good company. I mentioned in chapter 1 about how God gave us the gift and freedom to choose (providing we are using wisdom). When it comes to matters of the heart, we simply have two choices: (1) do it our way or (2) do it God's way. It doesn't take much mental effort to figure out God's way is the best. It may not feel like it is, but it is. I had to do this very thing. I had to surrender something I really wanted. I knew the Lord was telling me to let go of a man I thought I would marry. I shared a little already about the story in chapter 1. I had a dream one morning in the early part of 2010 that the path we were on God was not pleased. I heard a voice say that it would not last longer than three months. I remember feeling a lot of pain, and I saw the word *friends* above our heads. I woke from this dream thinking it was not of God (from the devil) and proceeded down the path I was warned not to take. In retrospect, God was clearly speaking to me. However, in my immature ability to hear and see God clearly, I missed the warning. Can I just say that if God is talking to you, listen and hear what he is saying and be obedient. It may just save you tears and a broken heart.

When I had the dream, my mistake was rationalizing with God. I remember saying to God, "It's so-and-so, he would not hurt me." Well, he did. I found out later, the dream was indeed accurate, and everything I saw in the dream came to pass. I made the mistake in believing more in this person than what God was trying to say to me. He was trying to spare me from being hurt again. God knows our hearts, our issues, and he knows what our future will look like and how it will play out. I should have trusted God and waited on him for the proper timing. In hindsight, we should have just remained friends and waited on God, whether the outcome was what I thought it to be or not. I wanted my dream of being married now, and I paid a price for that: a broken heart, disappointment, and broken dreams. In his sovereignty, God knew this would happen. However, he healed my heart and restored my ability to hope again and gave me a new dream. After this experience, God had my attention. I was determined to do it his way and in his timing. I encourage you to do the same. You may wrestle with the waiting process, but it will be fine eventually.

Barrenness

Have you ever felt like the promise of marriage has eluded you, felt delay, felt like life is passing you by and wonder if the Lord had forgotten all about the plans he has for bringing the right mate in your life? What about the friends in your circle who have gone on to become married and have started their family? Perhaps at gatherings you feel like the third wheel, like something is missing. Have you felt restless, had sleepless nights filled with silent tears? What about close friends and family members that once shared excitement and believed with you for a spouse now singing a different tune, asking ridiculous things like "How come you are not dating… What about so-and-so?" They are now wondering what is going on with you. "Why are you not married?" I cannot tell you how many times I have had this question asked to me. At first I used to get irritated by the question, as if I have control over the timing of the Lord. But now, my responses range from a smile and say nothing, and other times I would say, "I don't know, why don't you ask the Lord." Have you spent your time in waiting, contending with

God? I'm convinced that God sees purpose in the process. Why? Because your relationship with him becomes more strong, close, and more intimate. He becomes not just your father, husband, and provider, but a close friend, a confidant, the person who you can tell anything and everything to, and you don't have to worry if he will betray your trust or confidence. It becomes a reciprocal relationship. You get to know God better, and he gets to know you. You're building something here. You begin to enjoy him, and he enjoys you. In fact, God delights over us. We are his daily delight. He sings over us. He rejoices with us (Zephaniah 3:17). In my personal experiences, I had found that my barrenness in this area of my life brought me closer to the Lord. I had discovered intimacy with the Lord, a closeness that cannot even be compared to a relationship with a spouse.

Doing Good

Waiting on God is not just sitting by the wayside, doing nothing, and being passive. No, it is relentlessly hoping against hope even when it looks like there is no reason to hope. When people begin to tell you "maybe you should…" Be careful the sounds of compromising and settling are not too far behind. Doing good means that you are pursuing the things that God has called you to do, serving in the ministries he has appointed you, all the while not giving up your patience, hope, and faith that what God has for you will come. You may have days that are downcast. You may also grow a little weary. Remember, hope deferred does make the heart sick (Proverbs 13:12). I caution you to be on guard on these days. I heard someone say that between the prayer and *amen* and the time it takes for the promise to come, it seems impossible. I have learned that God does not want us to see the paths coming together. He does not want us to see the connections. If he showed us all of this, then it would not be faith. Without faith it is impossible to please him (Hebrews 11:6), and faith is the substance of things hoped for and the evidence of things not seen (Hebrews 11:1). It takes faith to endure and trust in God's promises. Without it, we cannot please God. Elijah waited for it to rain after he had declared that it would not rain for several years in Samaria (1 Kings 17, 18:1–46). Elijah went to the top of Mount Carmel, bent down to the ground, and put his face between his knees and prayed. Seven times Elijah sent his servant back to look towards the sea. On the seventh time, the servant reported that a cloud as small as a man's hand was rising from the sea (1 Kings 18:1–46). Elijah demonstrated persistence. He did not give up and was confident that God would do what he said he would do.

Walking in supernatural faith is hard on the natural eyes. There is a battle to reconcile true reality. You have to reconcile what God said and what you see in the natural. I had to do this. I believed God, especially since he confirmed his promises to me in his word (2 Corinthians 1:20). The struggle was with my natural eyes. There would be times after a church service when I would make a straight line to my car only to go home, close the door to my room, and cry in agony, frustration, and desperation. Learning to wait on God was brutal for me. Perhaps you can relate to this struggle. You are not alone, and let me tell you, God understands and can handle the questions, the struggling, and wrestling that come as a result of this process. When we choose to wait on God and trust him for his timing, these sorts of things come with the process. In retrospect, there was a purpose in the waiting. The pain and suffering were not in vain or wasted. I exhort you. Put God in remembrance (Isaiah 43:26) of his plans and promises for your life.

One morning I heard the Holy Spirit say to me, "Let us fixed our eyes on Jesus the author and perfecter of our faith who for the joy set before him endured the cross scorning it's shame and sat down at the right hand of the throne of God. Consider him who endured such opposition from sinful men, so that you will not grow weary and lose heart" (Hebrews 12:2–3). The Holy Spirit in essence was saying, "Do not focus on the suffering, the pain, restlessness, the faces that are judging you with their eyes, but focus on the promise, focus on the end, and anticipate the breakthrough, expect the breakthrough." There is a song I would hear. It's by Hillsong. It's titled "Turn Your Eyes on Jesus." Some of the lyrics caught my attention, "Turn your eyes upon Jesus, look for his wonderful face, and the things of the earth will grow strangely dim in the light of his glory and grace." This song was an answer to my prayers. I was saying to God, "Now that I know you will do it, how do I get my natural eyes to align with my spiritual eyes?" I needed help, and I needed it fast if I was to continue the walk of faith until the promise came to pass. You may ask, How do I turn my eyes upon Jesus, who is not tangible? What does that look like? Well, this is what he showed me. First, worship and praise him. This is your key to victory. Without worship and praise, you subject yourself to living life on the devil's playground. Stay in an attitude of prayer, praise, and worship. This is where God dwells. Whatever you are waiting on God for, these are your keys to keeping your eyes on Jesus. I encourage you to get a picture from God and let that picture be your guide in your journey of waiting. I end this section with Galatians 6:9, "Let us not become weary in doing good, for at the proper time we will reap a harvest if we do not give up" (NIV).

Trust the Timing of God

You may wonder if God's promises will ever come to pass. Sometimes waiting for what has been shown in the secret place (spiritual) to be manifest in the natural requires faith and patience—yes, faith and patience working side by side. I have found that you cannot obtain the promises of God without one or the other. If nothing is happening, then it is simply not the time. God is not slow, and he is not clueless. He knows what he is doing. Marriage is not like buying a pair of shoes that you can return if it does not fit properly or you decide you no longer want it. The timing of God is perfect, and we must learn to wait on him. He sees things which we are not aware of. He works from a different perspective. He works behind the scenes, and he sees so far ahead of what we cannot see. His perspective takes in the whole picture; we only have a snapshot in a space called time. He knows how to connect the right person at the right time. If we go ahead of him and do our own thing or rush the timing, it will be all wrong, not right. The frustrations you are experiencing while waiting on him in your singleness would be nothing in comparison to being married to someone that was not in God's timing. I have seen this too many times. Couples say "I do" and, days, weeks, months, years later, pay a price for what seemed good at the time (Proverbs 14:12). Some of those marriages eventually ended in divorce; others who are still married are not satisfied, not fulfilled, have conflict and struggles to overcome. This is not what God intended, and I have learned from other people's unfortunate experiences. There have been many times in which I was so restless and impatient that even if I wanted to go do my own thing, I could not. I knew if I did anything contrary to God's will, I would suffer the consequences of my choices. I was more afraid of the consequences than my inability to wait. I couldn't do anything but wait on God.

God works out of sight. He sometimes gives you a glimpse of the future, but it still requires faith to walk out. During my time of waiting on God, I was trying to piece together the things he would show me. No matter how I tried, it did not make sense; logic and reason were not helpful. I found myself meditating on Hebrew 11:1, "Faith is the substance of things hoped for and the evidence of things not seen." I was walking this passage out. Nothing that the Lord showed me in the spirit looked like anything in the natural. It was not easy to wait on God. Be that it may, in the end, the timing of God would be beautiful. As the writer of Ecclesiastes 3:11 states, "He makes all things beautiful in His timing." Get it? His timing, not ours. If you can wait, it will be worth it. Hope does not disappoint and, in some translations, hope does not put us to shame (Romans 5:5). The blessings of the Lord make one rich, and he adds no sorrow to it (Proverbs 10:22). As I reflect over my life, I cannot believe I went through so much as a result of being in dysfunctional relationships with men who had unresolved emotional wounds. Those experiences had changed me for the better, into a more wise, strong, and mature person. There were many lessons that I learned that I don't think I would have learned except by experiencing it firsthand. People who have unresolved emotional wounds make you feel like something is wrong with you. They dump their wounds and then move on, leaving you feeling dejected, rejected—you fill in the blanks. And sometimes, the situation is more difficult when people don't apologize, ask for forgiveness or take responsibility for their own actions. The lesson I learned is to take better care of myself by loving myself enough to not allow any dysfunction, dumping, or owning of people's issues in my life. In retrospect, every time I experienced a broken heart, only God could have healed me and bring me to a place of wholeness and maturity. This is why it is so important that we wait on him. You will pay the price emotionally and spiritually when you do not wait on Him. If I had the wisdom I have now then, I would have made better choices. I would have waited on God and not dated at all. God knows who our spouses are, and he knows how to connect the paths. If we get busy doing what he tells us to do, being obedient and willing, his word states we will eat the good of the land (Isaiah 1:19), and no good thing will he withhold from him who walks upright (Psalm 84:11).

Walking on Water

One day, I was at my spiritual father's house, and while I was talking to his wife, my spiritual father later shared that the Holy Spirit said that I would have a decision to make, and it would require me to walk on water. My spiritual father asked me what decision was I going to have to make. Initially, I could not think of anything, but then the more I pondered on the question, I thought maybe it had something to do with my standing in faith: waiting for God to bring the promise to pass. I was at a turning point. I needed to make a choice to either continue to stand or walk the other way. You see my faith was struggling at that point in time and I was ready to give up. Matthew 14:25–29 talks about when Jesus (during the fourth watch of the night) went out to meet the disciples. When the disciples saw him walking on water, they were afraid, but Peter said, "Lord, if it is you, tell me to come on the water." What did the Lord say? He told him to come. In some aspects, seasons of my life felt so much like this passage. I heard a word from the Lord, and he had confirmed it in his word. However, everything in the spiritual did not look anything like what I was seeing in the natural. I wrestled with this, and I wondered for a long time if what I was seeing and hearing were from God or from Satan, whose job is to deceive, steal, kill, and destroy. I also was aware that the heart was deceitful (Jeremiah 17:9). As I close this chapter, when you make a decision to walk on the water with Jesus, it does not mean that God will show you everything. You take a risk because the outcome of the promise may not look like you think. Nevertheless, trust him and not what you think the outcome of the promise will be like. Remember, his ways are not your ways and his thoughts are not your thoughts (Isaiah 55:8-9). No matter the outcome, all God's promises are yes and amen (2 Corinthians 1:20).

CHAPTER 9

Final Words of Encouragement

> "Being confident of this very thing,
> that he which hath begun a good work in you will
> perform it until the day of Christ Jesus."
>
> —Philippians 1: 6 (KJV)

In this final chapter, I will share passages (from God's lips to my ears) that were a personal lifeline on the days, weeks, months, and years when I felt discouraged and when it seemed like there was no end in this journey called waiting. I want you to know that there is a reality of hearing from God in moments of waiting. God hears your prayers and sees your cries. He is not clueless, distant, or hardened to your journey. In fact, he is in the journey with you, whether you see or experience him or not. I can say with confidence that God has been faithful to me in what seemed like one obstacle after another. Remember what I shared in chapter 3? God used each of these obstacles to perfect, to mature, and to teach me about the journey of waiting. March 12, 2008, I passed the California state exams to obtain my license as a marriage and family therapist

(LMFT). November 11, 2010, I completed my PhD dissertation and graduated. You may be wondering, what about the husband? Well, I would love to end this book with a perfect, romantic fairy-tale story about how I met the husband God always had in mind for me and paint this Happy Ever After, but the reality is that is currently not the case. Perhaps one day when it happens, I'll tell about it in another book, a sequel to this book! Nevertheless, though I am still waiting, there is another happy-ever-after story that I discovered. And that is I finally found true love, not in the arms of a man, but in all the right places, myself and Jesus! This happy ending may be a different twist from what is a typical happy-ever-after story. Personally, I think it is an even better ending. I will say that God's promises are a sure thing, and his word is forever settled in heaven. I don't know what God knows. All I know is what he has said and promised me in his word. I trust that, in the fullness of His timing, all things will be made beautiful.

In closing, I want you to know or remind some of you what you may already know: God is a covenant-keeping God, and anyone who trusts in him will never be put to shame (Romans 10:11, NIV). I pray that these passages will encourage and sustain you in your time of waiting on the Lord. Keep your dignity. Do not compromise your standards. Do not settle because you are tired of waiting. For some of you, the journey to the altar will be smooth sailing, while for others arduous and uncertain. Nevertheless, we all have to put in our time of waiting. I cannot tell you how long you will have to wait. For some, the wait may not be long, and for others, it may seem like an eternity. You may not have to wait as long as I had to wait. This was my own personal journey that was tailored specifically for me. However long the wait, remember God is always faithful to his promises. Allow the following passages to encourage, strengthen, and lead you in your journey of waiting. God's word is a lamp unto your feet, a light unto your path (Psalm 119:105).

God's Promises

> God is not a man that he should lie, nor a son of man that he should change his mind. Does he speak and then not act? Does he promised and not fulfill? (Numbers 23:19, NIV)

> May the Lord, the God of your fathers, increase you a thousand times and bless you as he has promised. (Deuteronomy 1:11)

> Wait on the Lord; be of good courage, and he shall strengthen thine heart: wait, I say, on the Lord. (Psalms 27:14)

> In your light, I see light. (Psalms 36:9)

> Why are you downcast, O my soul? Why so disturbed within me? Put your hope in God, for I will yet praise him, my Savior and my God. (Psalms 42:5, NIV)

> God is faithful and his word is tied to his testimony. (Psalm 119:38)

> Forever, O Lord they word is settled in heaven. (Psalm 119:89, KJV)

> They that sow in tears shall reap in joy. (Psalms 126:5, KJV)

> He will perfect that which concerns you. (Psalm 138:8, AMP)

You hem me in-behind and before; you have laid your hand upon me. (Psalms 139:5)

Finish your outdoor work and get your fields ready, after that build your house. (Proverbs 24:27, NIV)

He makes everything beautiful in its time. (Ecclesiastes 3:11, NIV)

The grass withers and the flowers fall, but the word of the God stands forever. (Isaiah 40:8, NIV)

One morning the Lord woke me up and I heard, "I will strengthen and harden you to difficulties."
    So do not fear, for I am with you; do not be dismayed, for I am your God. I will strengthen you and help you; I will uphold you with my righteous right hand. (Isaiah 40:10)

He giveth power to the faint; and to them that have no might he increaseth strength. Even youths shall faint and be weary, and the young men shall utterly fall: But they that wait upon the Lord shall renew their strength; they shall mount up with wings as eagles; they shall run, and not be weary, and they shall walk, and not faint. (Isaiah 40:31, NIV)

God's wisdom will be justified....those who hope in me will not be disappointed. (Isaiah 49:23, NIV)

FINAL WORDS OF ENCOURAGEMENT

For my thoughts are not your thoughts, neither are your ways my ways, declares the Lord. As the heavens are higher than the earth, so are my ways higher than your ways and my thoughts than your thoughts. (Isaiah 55:8–9)

So shall my word be that goeth forth out of my mouth. It shall not return unto me void, but it shall accomplish that which I please and it shall prosper in the thing whereto I sent it. (Isaiah 55:11, KJV)

Arise, shine, for your light has come. (Isaiah 60:1)

To bestow on them a crown of beauty instead of ashes, the oil of gladness instead of mourning, and a garment of praise instead of a spirit of despair. (Isaiah 61:3)

Do I bring to the moment of birth and not give delivery? says the Lord. (Isaiah 66:9)

The Lord said to me, you have seen correctly, for I am watching to see that my word is fulfilled. (Jeremiah 1:12, NIV)

The Lord replied: write down the revelation and make it plain on tablets so that a herald may run with it. For the revelation awaits an appointed time; it speaks of the end and will not prove false. Though it linger, wait for it; it will certainly come and will not delay. (Habakkuk 2:2–3, NIV)

Seek ye first the kingdom of God and all those things shall be added. (Matthew 6:33)

A farmer went out to sow his seed. As he was scattering the seed, some fell along the path, and the birds came and ate it up. Some fell on rocky places, where it did not have much soil. It sprang up quickly, because the soil was shallow. But when the sun came up, the plants were scorched, and they withered because they had no root. Other seed fell among the thorns, which grew up and choked the plants, so that they did not bear grain. Still other fell on good soil. It came up, grew and produced a crop, multiplying thirty, sixty, or even a hundred times. Then Jesus said: He who has ears to hear, let him hear. (Mark 4:3–9)

For with God nothing is impossible. (Luke 1:37)

Blessed is she who has believed that what the Lord has said to her will be accomplished. (Luke 1:45)

Then Jesus told him, because you have seen me, you have believed; blessed are those who have not seen and yet have believed. (John 20:29)

And calleth those things which be not as though they were. (Romans 4:17, KJV)

FINAL WORDS OF ENCOURAGEMENT

I have the mind of Christ and do hold the thoughts, feelings and purposes of his heart. (1 Corinthians 2:16, AMP)

For all the promises of God in him are yea, and in him Amen, unto the glory of God by us. (2 Corinthians 1:20, KJV)

Now thanks be unto God, which always causeth us to triumph in Christ. (2 Corinthians 2:14)

We are pressed on every side, but not crushed; perplexed, but not in despair, persecuted, but not abandoned; struck down, but not destroyed. (2 Corinthians 4:8–9)

Therefore we do no lose heart. Though outwardly we are wasting away, yet inwardly, we are being renewed day by day. For our light and momentary troubles are achieving for us an eternal glory that far outweighs them all. So we fix our eyes not on what is seen, but on what is unseen. For what is seen is temporary, but what is unseen is eternal. (2 Corinthians 4:16–18)

We live by faith, not by sight. (2 Corinthians 5:7, NIV)

And let us not be weary in well doing: for in due season we shall reap, if we faint not. (Galatians 6:7–9, KJV)

I pray that out of his glorious riches he may strengthen you with power through his Spirit in your inner being. (Ephesians 3:16)

Therefore do not be foolish, but understand what the Lord's will is. (Ephesians 5:17, NIV)

Now unto him that is able to do exceedingly abundantly above all that we ask or think according to the power that worketh in us. (Ephesians 3:20 KJV)

Being confident of this, that he who began a good work in you will carry it on to completion until the day of Christ Jesus. (Philippians 1:6, KJV)

Forgetting what is behind and straining toward what is ahead, I press on toward the goal to win the prize for which God has called me heavenward in Christ Jesus. (Philippians 3:13–14)

I can do all things through Christ which strengtheneth me. (Philippians 4:13, KJV)

We do not want to become lazy, but imitate those who through faith and patience inherit what has been promised. (Hebrews 6:12)

And so after waiting patiently, Abraham received what was promised. (Hebrews 6:15)

For God did this so that, by two unchangeable things in which it is impossible for God to lie, we who have fled to take hold of the

FINAL WORDS OF ENCOURAGEMENT

hope offered to us may be greatly encouraged. (Hebrews 6:18)

Cast not away therefore your confidence, which hath great recompense of reward. For ye have need of patience, that after ye have done the will of God, ye might receive the promise. For yet a little while, and he that shall come will come, and will not tarry. Now the just shall live by faith: but if any man draws back, my soul shall have no pleasure in him. (Hebrews 10:35–38)

Now faith is the substance of things hoped for, the evidence of things not seen. (Hebrews 11:1, KJV)

Now faith is being sure of what we hope for and certain of what we do not see. (Hebrews 11:1, NIV)

And without faith, it is impossible to please God. (Hebrews 11:6, NIV)

Let us fix our eyes on Jesus, the author and perfecter of our faith, who for the joy set before him endured the cross, scorning its shame, and sat down at the right hand of God. Consider him who endured such opposition from sinful men, so that you will not grow weary and lose heart. (Hebrews 12:2–3)

No discipline seems pleasant at the time, but painful. Later on, however, it produces a harvest of righteousness and peace for those who have been trained by it. (Hebrews 12:7–11)

After you have suffered a little while, will himself restore you and make you strong, firm and steadfast. (1 Peter 5:10)

The Lord is not slow in keeping his promises. (2 Peter 3:9)

And this is the confidence that we have in him that is we ask anything according to his will, he hears us. (1 John 5:14–15)

They overcame him by the blood of the Lamb and by the word of their testimony. (Revelation 12:11)

BIBLIOGRAPHY

American Association Christian Counselors (2016). *Find a Christian counselor.* Retrieved from http://www.aacc.net/resources/find-a-counselor/

Confucious. (n.d.). *Wisdom quotes.* Retrieved from http://www.brainyquote.com/quotes/authors/c/confucius_2.html

Dictionary.com. (2016). *Wait.* Retrieved from http://dictionary.reference.com/browse/wait?s=t

House, K. (2012, September 28). National poll confirms Americans spend a lot of time in lines. *The Oregonian.* Retrieved from: http://www.oregonlive.com/living/index.ssf/2012/09/national_poll_confirms_america.html

Lange, L. (2014). *Teachings: Forgiving ourselves and forgiving others.* Retrieved from: http://www.lifeapplicationministries.org/Session4a.htm and http://www.lifeapplicationministries.org/Session4.htm

Mathias, A. (2005). *Biblical foundations of freedom: Destroying satan's lies with God's truth.* Anchorage, Alaska: Wellspring Publishing.

Merriam Webster Online dictionary. (2015). *Wait.* Retrieved from http://www.merriam-webster.com/dictionary/wait

Murdock, N. L. (2009). *Theories of counseling: A case approach* (2nd ed.). Upper Saddle River, New Jersey: Pearson Education, Inc.

National Survey of Family Growth. (2012). *First marriages in the Unites States: Data from the 2006-2010 National Survey of Family Growth.* Retrieved from http://www.cdc.gov/nchs/data/nhsr/nhsr049.pdf

Smith, S. Y. (2010). *A phenomenological study of the impact of personal expectations on personal experiences of marriage and divorce.* Retrieved from ProQuest Dissertations database. (UMI No. 3427800)

Stone, A. (2012, August 18). Why waiting is torture. The *New York Times.* Retrieved from: http://www.nytimes.com/2012/08/19/opinion/sunday/why-waiting-in-line-is-torture.html?pagewanted=all

Wilson, S. D. (2001). *Hurt people, hurt people: Hope and healing for yourself and your relationships.* Grand Rapids, MI: Discovery House Publishers

Yen, H. (2011, August 25). United States divorce rate: 2009 Census Report reveals startling marriage trends. *Huffington Post.* Retrieved from http://www.huffingtonpost.com/2011/08/25/united-states-divorce-rat_n_935938.html

ABOUT THE AUTHOR

Dr. Shanda Smith grew up hearing about Jesus ever since she was a child in her grandfather's Baptist church in Little Rock, Arkansas. It was not until she and her family moved from Arkansas to California when Jesus began to pursue her heart. She accepted Jesus into her life at the age of 24. She has been a committed believer of Christ for twenty-one years and counting. Dr. Smith, who holds a PhD in General Psychology with an emphasis in Teaching, is a California licensed marriage and family therapist and a national certified counselor. She practices as a spirit-filled Christian therapist, is an assistant professor of counseling and family studies and faculty advisor at Liberty University in their online master degree programs. Dr. Smith currently lives in Southern California.

CPSIA information can be obtained
at www.ICGtesting.com
Printed in the USA
LVHW040735030323
740662LV00001B/203